T5-BBP-783

Eric Ravilious

Memoir of an Artist

Helen Binyon

Foreword by
Sir John Rothenstein

Introduction by
Richard Morphet

Frederic C. Beil
New York

Withdrawn from

Cleveland Inst. of Art Library

*Decoration for the 'Contents' page of **The Natural History of Selborne** by Gilbert White (The Nonesuch Press, 1938). Engraved on wood.*

N
6797
.R3
BS
1983

First published in the United States of America in 1983 by
Frederic C. Beil, Publisher
321 East 43rd Street
New York, N.Y. 10017

Text copyright © Helen Binyon 1983
Volume copyright © Bettina Tayleur Ltd 1983
Produced by Bettina Tayleur Ltd
1 Newburgh Street, London W1V 1LH

L.C.C. No 83–71366
ISBN 0–913720–42–9

Typesetting in Garamond by Input Typesetting Ltd, London
Picture reproduction by Imago Publishing Ltd, Thame, Oxon.
Printed and bound by South China Printing Co, Hong Kong
All rights reserved

Editor: Simon Rendle
Design: Grant Gibson
Research: Anthony Eyre

Contents

Foreword

Sir John Rothenstein

This book will surely afford widespread pleasure: Eric Ravilious remains one of the most ardently admired members of a generation marked by outstanding talent, and Helen Binyon, a fellow-student and intimate friend until the end of his life, was by far the best qualified person to write it. Regrettably she died before its publication.

Within an hour of his arrival at the Royal College of Art – to which he had been awarded a scholarship by the Eastbourne School of Art – Ravilious met Helen Binyon and Edward Bawden, also new arrivals. Within that hour or so his friendship with them both was firmly established. Both he and Bawden were assigned to the Design School to take their diplomas in book illustration; their friendship became ever closer. The art evolved by each of them was highly original, yet it had enough in common to enable them when occasion arose to work in close concert.

At the Royal College Ravilious was soon accorded a place among fellow-students of exceptional talent, including Henry Moore, Bawden, Albert Houthuesen, John Piper and Percy Horton. Ravilious's accomplished versatility delighted my father, then principal at the College, who also particularly liked him. I well remember his expressing his admiration for Ravilious, and this at a time when the college was attended by so considerable a number of students of conspicuous ability.

Owing to my parents keeping 'open house' on Sunday evenings during term for the students I had the privilege of coming to know a number of them, including Ravilious, Rav or the Boy as fellow-students called him, considering that the name Eric did not suit him. Friendly we immediately became but owing to the wholly different circumstances of our lives we rarely met. When we did, however, he was warm and candid, discussing works of art he had seen on his frequent visits to the Victoria and Albert Museum, certain departments of which he might already have been serving as a professional guide, such was the range of his knowledge. He discussed much else, including people whom he knew. Among these there must have been some whom he neither liked nor approved of, for his own standards of conduct were scrupulous, yet I cannot recall his uttering a critical word about anyone. His attention was focussed rather on friends and acquaintances whose work he admired, whose company he enjoyed. Later on I became aware of a similarity in his attitude to his fellow men and women and the subjects he selected to represent. Instead, as many artists do, of accepting subjects come upon more or less by chance, or enobling the ugly, he selected those which evoked his particular admiration, whether on the South Downs or, as a war artist, Arctic landscapes and flying boats.

Not many years after they left the Royal College the memorable opportunity came to him and Bawden to work on a major project, the decoration of the Refreshment Room at Morley College, Lambeth. The paintings, among the most notable British murals of the time, were begun in 1928, completed some two years later and 'opened' by Stanley Baldwin – only to be destroyed, during the Blitz. These works I had the privilege of seeing, and clearly recall how deeply impressive they were.

My father – one of those consulted by the Principal of Morley College, Mrs Hubback – suggested that subjects from Shakespeare would be appropriate. 'Bawden and Ravilious,' he wrote in the third volume of *Men and Memories*, 'accordingly made a series of designs from Shakespeare's plays, also from some of the earlier miracle-plays. These they carried out beautifully on the distempered walls, first drawing the outlines freely, with so sensitive a touch one almost regretted they would not so remain. Happily, in adding colour they showed no less perfect workmanship.' The Morley College paintings evoked ardent admiration and their destruction, long felt regret.

The range of Ravilious's work was extraordinarily wide, spanning watercolour painting, wood engraving, lithography, and design in the fields of ceramics, glass, furniture, textiles and advertising. He also served as an Official War Artist, making a number of memorable works while attached to the Royal Marines, before his premature death in Iceland at the age of only thirty-nine. Had Ravilious lived to twice that age the extent of his creativity, always scrupulous, often inspired, would have been extraordinary. Its quality and variety are treated by Helen Binyon with admirable discernment.

Eric Ravilious photographed by Serge Chermayeff, Autumn 1939.

5

Preface

It may seem that this book is somewhat overburdened with introductory paragraphs, but we felt that in the sad absence of Helen Binyon herself we should launch her book with suitable fanfares.

It is five years now since Helen first arrived in my office with the manuscript of the book. She had come on the kind recommendation of Joseph Darracott of the Imperial War Museum. I was captivated by her text and by the wealth of Ravilious material she brought with her, and willingly agreed to try and help her bring *Eric Ravilious: Memoir of An Artist* to publication. It was a slow process for it seemed far too many publishers had forgotten, if they ever knew, Eric Ravilious's contribution to beautiful book design and illustration. Barely a year later we were tragically interrupted by the news of Helen's illness. Her letter telling me of this was remarkable, full of plans for the book, her frustration at not being able to see new exhibitions, in particular one of Ravilious's war paintings at the Imperial War Museum, and it did not contain a trace of self pity. She died shortly afterwards and I became even more determined that her book, a labour of love, should see the light of day. What follows is her own 'Preface', and I should like to join her in thanking the many people who have made the publication of her book possible.

Bettina Tayleur, February 1983

My aim in writing this book has been to record the range of Eric Ravilious's work, to give an idea of its qualities, and to show something of what it was like to know him, as remembered by his friends and as reflected in his many letters to them.

Eric was lost in Iceland, where he went as a war artist in 1942. He was thirty-nine years old. His wife, Tirzah, died ten years later. His three children, John, James and Anne, have lent me all the family papers and records, and it was at their suggestion that I have written the book. Although so distant, his friends' memories of him are still very vivid, and I have quoted largely from what they have written or told me. I would like to express my gratitude to them for their invaluable help and to thank them here.

Helen Binyon

Peggy Angus, Edward Bawden, Mr & Mrs Douglas Percy Bliss, Henry Boys, Jennifer Carey, Noel Carrington, Olive Cook, Joseph Darracott, Clifford Ellis, Edmund Gray, Nicolete Gray, Mrs Evelyn Hepher, Andrew Higgens, Mrs Margaret Higgens, Howard & Julia Hodgkin, John Lake, Ariane Lewis, John O'Connor, James Ravilious, John Ravilious, Simon Rendle, Sir James Richards, Diana Saintsbury-Green, Cecilia Lady Sempill, Riette Sturge-Moore, Arthur Tooth & Sons Ltd, Donald Towner, R. C. Tuely, Anne Ullmann, Barry & Sariah Viney, Geoffrey Wales, The Wedgwood Trust, A. Zwemmer Ltd.

Eric Ravilious and Helen Binyon

Richard Morphet

Deputy Keeper, Modern Collection, The Tate Gallery

The work of Eric Ravilious has always been appreciated and enjoyed, but as time passes it becomes increasingly clear that his stature was greater than has often been admitted. After a period in which considerations of style and genre have loomed disproportionately large, there is now widespread appreciation again of the central importance of content in art. This is propitious for an understanding of Ravilious's work and of the close unity between all its parts – a main theme of this book, which considers Ravilious equally as a fine and as an applied artist.

Most of Ravilious's work was small in scale and its medium was either delicate or supportive of a text or a manufactured object. In all these fields his approach was broadly traditional, and his work addressed neither political and social issues nor (in any direct way) the avant-garde contest of his period between Surrealism and abstraction. None of these facts, however, necessarily connotes a marginal position within the British art of his day, or a lesser contribution to it. Every idea has its own just form and Ravilious found his. Those who open themselves to what Ravilious expresses through his various disciplines will find a sensibility linked in complex ways to the principal currents in the art of his day. And although they will find appearances translated onto a flat surface with extraordinary vividness, they will discover too that Ravilious penetrates beneath the surface of things in a meditation on the mystery of their nature and existence, and on their location in space and time. Like all significant art, that of Ravilious has an outer and an inner reality.

His work is orderly, precise and full of specific detail. From the early 1930s this characteristic is paradoxically united in his watercolours with distinct breadth of design (as it frequently is, in all his media, with breadth of the scene evoked). In his landscapes the curve and bulk of the earth are conveyed with an almost physical feel and where there are paths, bridges or causeways one is led in imagination along them into the deep space of the picture, step by step, with a verifiable, seemingly tangible sense of actuality. These qualities coexist with a beautiful assertion of the medium itself of watercolour, as a deposit on the paper. Carefully composed, Ravilious's watercolours nevertheless convey a strong sense of the spontaneity of an actual moment of observation. This combination of breadth with immediacy recalls Cotman whom he is known to have admired and more generally places him centrally in the English watercolour tradition, as do his powerful sense of the land and its occupation and, no less, of the sky, the weather and their frequent moistness. But Ravilious often seems still more English because unlike most well-known English artists of this generation he hardly ever went abroad, and virtually his only significant non-English subjects concern the defence of Britain by air and sea.

The mix in Ravilious's art of peculiarly English scenes with

Abstract decoration for J. M. Dent's Everyman series, 1936–7. Engraved on wood.

nineteenth- and twentieth-century machinery places it also within a wide-spread tendency of interwar Western art as a whole, namely the examination of an artist's own national or local scene; the best-known example is American Regionalism. Characteristic of such art was the use of traditional and comprehensible pictorial styles. Looking back as he did to pre-modern sources, Ravilious shows no trace of the sensuousness and solidity in paint handling so important to many English artists in the work of the masters of Post-Impressionism, but his interest in concise and accessible imagery links him both with the Camden Town artists (he met Ginner), with his friend Percy Horton, with his near-contemporaries in the Euston Road School, and with the work of a poet close to them, W. H. Auden. Ravilious's observation of the everyday scene and of the odd details of English life also overlapped in the late 1930s with Mass Observation, while his subject matter and his concern with precision connect his work with that of Tristram Hillier and especially of Edward Wadsworth (a letter from whom is printed on p. 107).

An important difference between Ravilious and the abstract, Surrealist and Euston Road artists of the 1930s was that he did not have a crusading attitude regarding the direction that art should take. Nevertheless, and despite his fundamental difference of aim from abstraction and Surrealism, it is not only with the Euston Road artists that his work shows links. In abstract art, for example, the role of feeling or mood is vital. In his engraved abstract devices Ravilious contrived simultaneously to accentuate bold and distinctive forms and to convey particular emotions difficult to define in words, while in all media his work shows a delight in strong, elementary shape, cleanly articulated and interacting with elegant, living line. This preoccupation reminds one repeatedly of the aesthetic of Ben Nicholson. Both artists responded enthusiastically to the crisp forms of nautical design (on which John Piper, a friend of Ravilious, wrote an article in 1938[1]), to imagery of kings, queens and fireworks, and to sports such as tennis and billiards in which precision was essential. In British art of the 1930s a continuum of sensibility links Nicholson's most abstract works with Ravilious's most figurative.

Although Ravilious's connection with Surrealism is less explicit, his work of the 1930s is peculiarly of its period and it is difficult to believe that the sense of latent drama in many of his scenes, devoid of inhabitants or with a single strange object or structure presiding over a landscape, would be quite as they are were it not for the Surrealists' discovery of a super reality in everyday life. Already before the establishment of Surrealism in England such an awareness was evident in the work of Ravilious's teacher, Paul Nash. The fact that it was joined in Nash with an obsession with design, with an interest in constructions seen in a landscape setting and with mastery of the English watercolour tradition shows how powerful an influence on Ravilious he must have had. The work of both conveys a sense of sudden revelation. This quality is apparent in a different guise in the work of another brilliant watercolourist whom Ravilious admired, David Jones. But Ravilious derives it more directly from Nash, with whom he shares a central preoccupation with the mystery of place, time and space – the spot and the moment seen in relation to a wider perspective. Despite Ravilious's greater 'straightforwardness' pictorially, he as well as Nash was an important contributor to the development of English Neo-Romantic landscape art. Wartime isolation from the continent intensified collective awareness of the English atmosphere and past.

These had long been central subjects of Ravilious's art, though the element of distortion which began to be prominent in Neo-Romanticism from around the time of his death is alien to his work. His affinities with Samuel Palmer and with Henry Moore are dicussed below.

Comparison with the new art of the early and mid 1940s only accentuates the contrasting qualities in Ravilious of order, subtlety and a certain understatement. Though he contributed to the revival of interest in Victoriana his work shows more fundamental inspiration from the art of the eighteenth century, the century of Devis, Sandby and Stubbs and of kinds of art which combined keen observation with a certain detachment. Both qualities are strong in Ravilious, the latter perhaps to an unusual degree. All his work has an attractive warmth because it records or immediately anticipates human activity within the scene depicted. But this makes all the more remarkable the substantial absence of human beings from his pictures, particularly in his last ten years. Appearing largely through traces of their presence, they seem to be interpreted in terms of functions rather than of personality. When people do appear they tend to be either types (masked revellers, practitioners of specific trades), slightly doll-like (e.g. tennis players), actors, repeated units seen from afar, or (as in the zodiacal figures in the 1929 Almanack) concepts. Both in the delightfully-peopled Morley College murals and in *High Street* (two works containing many figures in settings), the objects seem to have more personality and presence than the human beings, who in *High Street* have minimal (or in many cases no) facial features. Perhaps this has something to do with the fact that, though filled with fun and with curiosity about life, Ravilious was also found by those who knew him to have a slightly elusive quality. J. M. Richards recalls that 'he never lost a kind of wariness against all allegiances and personal involvements'[2]. In his work, on the other hand, one senses a deep and intense involvement, but one with something more changeless than human relationships.

It is perhaps significant of this central quality in Ravilious's art that the same combination of absence of people with extra-worldly preoccupation is found in the art of Paul Nash[3]. Like that of Nash, Ravilious's art shows unusual awareness of time and space, yet at the same time suggests an inherent concern with matters of the imagination and of the spirit which lie beyond measurement. One of the most personal aspects of his work is its combination of such inward vision with the keen observation of matter-of-fact reality, which he makes us see with new delight. He finds poetry on both levels, and also in their inter-relation. We have already noted the satisfying and inviting way in which Ravilious plots out the precise position of elements in the near, middle and far distance of his watercolours; in doing this he leads us not only into a particular space but also into a special mental world. Whether the scene is indoors or out, one has an enhanced sense of time passing, from second to second. But Ravilious locates contemporary existence in a broader perspective. In many works, signs of modern life are juxtaposed with traces of prehistoric man. In others Ravilious reiterates the timeless cycle of the seasons and the activities which result from it, especially the fertility of harvest symbolized by ears and sheaves of corn. This is a central theme of Samuel Palmer, whom Ravilious further echoes in associating man's yearly round with an exceptional prominence of celestial bodies. The sphere of the sun is beautifully noticeable in many of his watercolours, and his wood engravings feature sun, moon, stars and comets set in looming proximity to

'July' from the Lanston Monotype Corporation's **Almanack 1929**.

implements and plants, recalling their closeness to man as they balance on the rim of Palmer's intimate valley[4]. Ravilious's zodiacal figures come right down into earthly situations – even into rooms – where they establish a magic presence. Vital though the verifiable world is in his art Ravilious often seems therefore to use symbols and selected natural phenomena to draw our awareness beyond material reality. Although this aspect of his work is not as obvious as in Nash or Jones its importance is underlined by noting at how many points his pictorial vocabulary overlaps with that of a third explicitly visionary artist of the time. In the work of Cecil Collins key Ravilious motifs such as lighthouses, prehistoric sites and fireworks are all important, while his *The Cells of Night* 1934 (Tate Gallery) visualises the inner spirit of man awakening beneath a sky whirling with meteors that seem strangely close to earth.

As Helen Binyon had special reason to know, it was in Sussex, with its austere and curving Downs, that these aspects of Ravilious's art found their greatest inspiration from the English landscape. It seems oddly appropriate, therefore, that it should have been for a site in that county, and when Ravilious's powers were at their height, that Henry Moore's carved stone *Recumbent Figure* 1938 was commissioned, a work much concerned with the spirit in landscape and with landscape as spirit. As Moore later recalled, 'It was then that I became aware of the necessity of giving outdoor sculpture a far-seeing gaze. My figure looked out across a great sweep of the Downs, and her gaze gathered in the horizon. The sculpture . . . became a mediator between modern home and ageless land'.[5] Ravilious was one with all these contemporary English artists in seeing man in a wider context than that of his immediate circumstances. It is not surprising that for all its acute observation of the actual scene his work, like that of Barnett Freedman, often gives the sensation of a dream, a state in which reality is often not so much denied as heightened.

Ravilious's success as both realist and poetic artist results from his basing each work on a clear and precise conception. There are no incidentals in his art; everything is excluded which does not support the

*Celebratory decoration for **The Hansom Cab and The Pigeons** by L. A. G. Strong (The Golden Cockerel Press, 1935). Engraved on wood.*

chosen theme. Though already remarkable his work of the 1920s is in general more detailed and elaborated than it became in his great last ten years. A change from relative density to a sparer yet stronger design, filled with a sense of air and light, seems to come first in the wood engravings (however compressed) and to be established in all his media by 1932. His use of colour was exceptionally effective partly because it was restricted to so few elements per work. Of key importance was his gift for selection, his eye for that which, amid millions of ordinary sights available to all, is somehow singular. Each such element – a cloud, a dustpan, the spiral in a Swiss roll – is picked out and remains distinctive even if its vehicle is an engraving into which many elements have to be packed. In the watercolours the beauty and the strangeness of things which might otherwise have been thought inconsequential are conveyed to us by their relative individual isolation. This is one reason why Ravilious's grasp of texture and tactility is so telling (as well as being so remarkable in so fluid a medium). Thrust into prominence, the texture of wood, grass or rust, the weave of net, racquet or corn sheaf, come alive on the sheet, and one can almost feel the chalk of the Down being cut into to form the image of a horse.

It was Ravilious's skill as a designer which, in each work afresh, enabled him to merge such specific perceptions into an effective whole. His design skill is that of a master, for leaping beyond mere admirable or striking composition he conjures from his component elements the instant evocation of a special mood. The tiniest tailpiece can evoke the passage of time, swift movement or the processes of growth. A design to celebrate a special occasion suggests at a glance the experience of past centuries, contemporary activity nationwide, and the prospect of marvellous spectacle. His much-loved fireworks link an earthly mood of this kind to an awareness of cosmic forces.

Ravilious's war work was of necessity done in conditions less conducive to the kind of compression, at once engaging and revelatory, which thus characterizes his work through the 1930s. Nevertheless his war pictures are among his finest achievements precisely because their important element of record and reportage is married with a grasp of atmosphere and environmental scale, and of man's relation to forces more enormous and permanent than those of an enemy in war. Without his more meditative researches of the interwar years, this would not have been possible. In all Ravilious's work observation and idea were united to remarkable effect. His early loss to British art was the more tragic because of his special ability to focus and celebrate the reality of the here and now while at the same time giving his art the wider imaginative and spiritual range which ensures increasing recognition of its stature.

The work of an outstanding artist enables later generations to come close to his personality in important respects, but there is a special value in the recollections of those who were close to him in life. Helen Binyon's vivid memoir is such a primary source. Not only does it contain a wealth of

11

factual information but it captures, as this necessarily detached introduction cannot, the liveliness and fun of Ravilious and his circle – qualities which go hand in hand in his art with those outlined above. It also indicates the continuing importance to him personally and professionally of several gifted contemporaries from his days at the Royal College of Art who are therefore hardly mentioned here. An exception, however, must be made of Helen Binyon herself. In her memoir Helen makes clear that she and Ravilious were students together at the Royal College and that they were friendly in the 1930s and till his death. Without being told, however, the reader would have no idea that in these later years their relationship was of great importance to them both. In a book with so strong a biographical emphasis it seems desirable to make this clear, and also to indicate how remarkable the author was in her own right.

Helen Binyon was born on 9 December 1904, the twin daughter of the poet and art historian Laurence Binyon (1869–1943) and his wife Cicely, née Powell. Since 1895 Binyon had worked in the Department of Prints and Drawings at the British Museum, of which he was ultimately the Keeper. He was also for many years Keeper of the Department of Oriental Prints and Drawings, and developed a pioneering interest in oriental paintings. No less fruitful was his influence on the appreciation of Blake, Girtin and Cotman, and of Francis Towne, whom he virtually 'discovered'. His own poetry was pervaded by a brooding love of the English earth and legends.[6] Educated at St Paul's Girls School, Helen Binyon entered the Design School of the Royal College of Art in the same year as Ravilious, 1922. The Principal, William Rothenstein, was a friend of Laurence Binyon's and it might be thought, as indeed was borne out by her career, that the practice of art was a natural and straightforward extension of Helen's background. Her years at the Royal College were however not without problems. From her mother's side of the family the influence was towards a conventional role in society. While at the Royal College she was presented at Court as well as leading, part of the time, the kind of social life consistent with this. The backgrounds of many of her fellow students were very different, not least those of the men, some of whom, moreover, were older because they had served in the war while others, such as Ravilious, Edward Bawden and Barnett Freedman, seemed to have unusual personalities. It seems, therefore, that while acquainted in general with Ravilious and his immediate circle, Helen Binyon did not get to know them well in these years and indeed felt a certain tension between the contrasting possibilities suggested by her own family background. Like Ravilious she was, however, taught by Paul Nash and his influence on her remained decisive.

In the years after the Royal College Helen Binyon spent one year in Paris and another in the United States, where she worked on the hand-colouring of reproductions of works by William Blake. Like all aspects of her work this depended on her gift for meticulous precision; in the same period she obtained a job as draughtsman at the College of Arms. Her own work as a graphic artist was in engraving and watercolour. As a wood engraver she exhibited at the Redfern Gallery as part of the same group as Nash and Ravilious. Her prints are remarkably close in feeling to those of Ravilious and her line engravings of the period bring out at least as strongly a very similar response to the singularity of individual *things*. As in Ravilious, objects or people do not overlap; the isolation of each permits its structure and its feel to be appreciated. An almost physical

Helen Binyon in the 1930s.

delight is conveyed in the coil of a rope, the lean and touch of a ladder, the slicing of a haystack and, precisely as in Ravilious, the sensation of crossing a bridge. Her watercolours of the 1930s show a steely line, exceptionally narrow and accurate, and much greater detail than her prints, allied to a fresh simplicity in the touch of the medium. The principal subjects are land – and townscape, with a special enjoyment of interrelated roofs, fences (a key Nash and Ravilious motif) and unpretentious village homes, some of them in Essex.

Her work as a book illustrator was first published in the 1920s. She contributed extremely Ravilious-like wood engravings to Maria Edgeworth's *Angelina, or L'Amie Inconnue* (The Swan Press, 1933), to her father's tiny *Brief Candles* (Golden Cockerel Press, 1938) and to the Penguin Illustrated Classics edition of *Pride and Prejudice*, also in 1938. Between 1940 and 1949 Oxford University Press published a series of at least ten books for children about two girls named Polly and Jane. These were written by Margaret Binyon and extensively illustrated by Helen. The illustrations make most effective use of their restriction to one or two colours each, and make maximum play with pattern and with varied and often minute texture. The overall effect of each illustration is of a bold and telling directness, within which the structure of any object depicted is examined with a degree of interest surprising in children's books, enhanced by the often striking angles of view adopted. The man picnicking on the beach in *A Day at the Sea* (1940) is a portrait of Ravilious. Helen's final book was *The Children Next Door* (Aladdin Books, New York, 1949), which she both illustrated and wrote. Here striking simplicity is taken still further, the material ranging from line drawings of shells to objects such as an open watercolour box viewed from directly above.

It was in about 1930 that Helen and Margaret Binyon, in creating a puppet show with which to welcome their father home from a visit to

*Frontispiece for Jane Austen's **Pride & Prejudice** (Penguin Illustrated Classics, 1938). Engraved on wood by Helen Binyon.*

*Ravilious as depicted in A **Day At The Sea** (Oxford University Press, 1940). The 'Binyon Books' were written by Margaret Binyon and illustrated by Helen.*

Japan, initiated the involvement with puppetry which will probably be seen as Helen's most lasting professional legacy. Their interest in puppets had been fired by seeing, as children, one of the legendary puppet performances given by William Simmonds (1876–1968). Oddly enough, Helen seems never to have met Simmonds, but her description of the special qualities of his puppetry pinpoints the values which always governed her own work in this medium, notwithstanding its increasing concern with innovation as the years went by. Simmonds's work, she wrote, achieved a 'rare and exquisite balance of the relationships between all the elements – the puppets were extraordinarily sensitively carved, jointed and moved; the content of the scene exactly the right weight for its puppet actors . . . the music of exactly the right delicacy for the size of the puppets. . . . The limitations the artist set himself . . . were a source of artistic unity and intensity. . . . The show, delicate and allusive, was pure enchantment'.[7]

Like Simmond's puppets, the Binyons' were marionettes. In the years after the Royal College Helen had learned wood carving as well as engraving at the Central School of Art. She designed the sets and made the puppets, while the words were written and spoken by Margaret (who had won a prize at one of the Oxford verse speaking competitions organized by John Masefield – Laurence Binyon, had for many years been much concerned with the revival of verse speaking). Throughout the 1930s the sisters gave performances of their portable puppet theatre all over England, under the name Jiminy Puppets, from 'gemini', the Latin word for twins. They were hired for private or charity shows, but also gave short public seasons. One of these was at the Poetry Bookshop, and in June 1938 they gave a six-night season at the Mercury Theatre with words by Montagu Slater and music by Benjamin Britten and Lennox Berkeley performed by the composers and others.[8] Jiminy Puppets aimed at beauty, fun and dramatic effect. They made much use of traditional British ballads and songs and (also in 1938) appeared on television with their performance of ''Twas on the Broad Atlantic'. Individual pieces lasted about four minutes, and an evening's performance about an hour. The sisters' last public performances (no longer under the name Jiminy) were seasons in Bristol in the early 1950s, but in July 1969 they gave a final private performance at a party in their own former home, the Keeper's House at the British Museum. This was to celebrate the centenary of their father's birth and included a play he had written for them about the Museum, in which an Egyptian mummy and other exhibits come alive and argue about their relative popularity with visitors. The setting of this performance was doubly appropriate as the house was then occupied by the specialist in eastern art, Basil Gray (Keeper of Oriental Antiquities) and his wife Nicolete, younger sister of Helen and Margaret and an important figure in the establishment of international modern art in Britain in the 1930s as well as a distinguished historian, teacher and designer of lettering.

The period around 1933 was one of great change in Helen Binyon's life. In that year both her sisters married and her parents left the British Museum. Helen moved into a flat in Belsize Park shared with a fellow student from the Royal College, Peggy Angus, an art teacher who was to become a very original designer of tiles, fabrics and wallpaper. Helen and her family and friends all considered her renewed friendship with Peggy at this time to have had a liberating effect on her. The antithesis of the more restricted and conventional side of Helen's family, Peggy was an

A wood engraving by Helen Binyon, printed in red on pale blue paper, announcing 'a new Puppet Show' to be presented by Margaret and Helen Binyon in Bristol.

extraordinary person. Their flat was decorated with large grey fronds cut from sheets of *The Times* and pasted onto a pink ground. They gave large and lively parties here and at Furlongs, Peggy's cottage on the South Downs (described in Helen's memoir) which she acquired in 1933. It was through Peggy that Helen (who was unusual in the circle in having a car) met Ravilious again and got to know him well. As recounted in the memoir the Raviliouses would come to stay at Furlongs, but in 1934 Ravilious and Helen fell very much in love. Ravilious used then to come alone to stay at Furlongs with Peggy and Helen. In 1938 Helen decided that distressing though this would be their intimate relationship should not continue. For the Raviliouses' sake as well as her own she could not agree that both relationships should coexist. She and Ravilious remained close friends, and his death reinforced her friendship with Tirzah Ravilious. She took an affectionate interest in the three Ravilious children and it was they who asked her to write the memoir which is published now.

Lennox Berkeley (left) and Benjamin Britten at the piano, with Margaret and Helen Binyon operating their puppets, 1938.

Helen Binyon and Eric Ravilious, drawn at Furlongs c1934 by Peggy Angus.

Ravilious's letters to Helen Binyon make clear the importance he attached to her views on his work, which he was always bringing for her to see. It is evident how much they had in common beyond many shared friendships. Both influenced formatively by Paul Nash, they drew inspiration together from the English watercolour tradition and from the sense of the genius loci. This is apparent in the watercolours in which, at this period, they were both particularly prolific and particularly interested in technical precision. They had both taken part in the 1920s revival of wood engraving and both were accustomed to solving problems of design for a large audience. Above all, though Ravilious's work is the more wide-ranging and profound, their work is very close in feeling. It seems inevitable and right that the work of both will be associated permanently.

In the first half of the war Helen worked for the Admiralty in Bath, drawing hydrographic charts; she was living in Bath when Ravilious died. Her later war work was in London preparing photographic exhibitions for the Ministry of Information and doing ambulance service in the evenings. Soon after the war there came another turning point in her life, when she began teaching at Bath Academy of Art, Corsham. Bath Academy included both a School of Visual Arts and a course for training teachers of art, drama and music in general education. Although Helen taught in both, her principal and increasing role was in the training of teachers. But her work was unusually rewarding because of the emphasis laid by Bath Academy's remarkable Principal, Clifford Ellis, on the importance of interaction between the two parts of the Academy and on the value of innovation. Helen was thus able to contribute not only as a teacher of drawing and watercolour and as a pioneer in her special field of puppetry but also, as a senior member of the staff, in the weekly criticisms of the work which students of all disciplines within the School of Visual Arts had produced in response to set projects. Her sense of the importance of observation and of the need for a work to convey a feeling of life rather than of mere formal experiment combined with her undoctrinaire attitude towards materials and style to make her a widely respected member of the team. As Clifford Ellis writes, 'Helen enjoyed being in this lively community and her contribution was one of the reasons why its work could not deteriorate into illiberal 'Basic Design' '.

After the personal loss and communal tribulation of the war, Helen's work at Corsham seems to have given her a new lease of life. At first she worked there part-time, sharing houses first in Hampstead with Peggy Angus and then with her sister Margaret and children in Bristol. When Helen became a full-time teacher at Corsham she bought an old weavers' cottage in the village. Her love of children and her vocation for teaching found their ideal fusion in the introduction of local primary school children to her own students, as part of teaching projects embracing both art, music and drama (of which puppetry is itself a synthesis). The ending of Helen's public appearances with marionettes coincided roughly with the development of her special interest in shadow puppets. This lay at the heart of her teaching at Corsham and culminated annually in public performances of shadow plays created by her students. Shadow puppets were also the perfect vehicle for Helen's teaching method, which in watercolour and puppetry alike centred on the setting up of situations within which students were encouraged simultaneously to explore their own sense of the materials employed and of the content to be expressed, so as to discover a personal solution rather than one dictated by narrow rules. In her Corsham productions there was thus a strong element of openness and surprise. She drew both on centuries-old traditions of East and West and on more recent cultures such as that of the Bauhaus, employing abstract imagery and exploring pure sound. Anything was admissible so long as the result was satisfying, thorough and complete. However brief, her puppet shows were always works of art.

Helen retired from Corsham in 1965 and with her twin sister bought a house in Chichester overlooking a garden which she created, bisected by a deeply-cut stream and with the city's tall and ancient flint wall as a backdrop. The insights of her Jiminy and Corsham years were summed up in her *Puppetry Today* (Studio Vista, 1966), described by Clifford Ellis as 'her testament as a teacher'. This book was trenchant in its criticism of poor standards and of slovenliness, but above all was positive and infectiously enthusiastic. It drew on Helen's wide experience of puppetry in other countries to give a clear account of the four main branches of the art – string, glove, rod and shadow puppets, with special emphasis on the last – but unlike many puppet books it was artistic as well as technical. Thus a central theme was the need to realize fully, and to integrate, all the different aspects of a puppet show – the construction of the puppets, of course, but also their precise design, so as to compress into each single form as complete as possible a sense of representation or identity; and above all their movement. The aim, she explained, should be not merely to illustrate a pre-existing story or score, but to allow the particular characters and capabilities of the puppets to bring it to life, so that theme and material should be one. Helen Binyon stressed that puppetry was not doll-making but drama, the work of art being not the puppets but the performance as a totality. Any material, however improbable, was acceptable, and sources of inspiration for movement which she cited included weather, kinetic art and the dance of Merce Cunningham.

Following the appearance of *Puppetry Today* Helen was commissioned by the Arts Council of Great Britain to undertake a survey of professional puppetry in England, and she presented this in 1971. Here the points made in her book gained added force by contrast with the generally low level of accomplishment she had found in viewing thirty-seven very varied puppet performances, but also found confirmation in the work of a very few young puppeteers, particularly Christopher Leith, as well as in such diverse directions as the American Bread and Puppet Theatre and Basil Brush at the London Palladium. Identifying puppetry's intermediate position between art, drama and dance, she stressed the need to combine the qualities of all three traditions. She wrote that 'what we *feel* must come from what we *see*' (rather than simply from what story we hear), and urged the establishment of a permanent formal link between puppetry and living dramatic art. Running through both this report and *Puppetry Today* is an exhilarating stress on the excitement of discovery and the rich potential of puppetry. Helen Binyon was fascinated by the scope for transformation offered not only by the individual puppet (where she delighted in ingenuities of every kind) but by the ability of a performance to conjure, for a brief, concentrated span, a complete and convincing world. Her writings have a lasting value deriving from a consistent clarity combined with a feeling for the magic of her art which seems to extend beyond puppetry (or watercolour) itself to an infectious response to the curiosity and beauty of the world around us.

Although not funded by the Arts Council, the Experimental Puppet Workshop which Helen led at the Central School of Speech and Drama in July–August 1973 realized one of the principal recommendations in her 1971 survey. As described in the resulting report it was 'a leap in the dark' made collectively by puppeteers, artists, theatre designers, poets, actors and musicians. It was attended by the Director of the National Theatre and ended on a note of optimism created by the sense of expanded possibility realized through a concentrated interdisciplinary approach, and by the appointment of Christopher Leith and Jennifer Carey, members of the Workshop, to the staff of the National Theatre.

The Experimental Workshop was Helen Binyon's last formal undertaking in puppetry, though she remained closely involved in the field. However, she continued till near the end of her life to paint in watercolour, especially when on holiday, for example in Provence, Sicily, Yugoslavia, Greece, Morocco and Tunisia. Her postwar work in this medium was much more free than during the years of her friendship with Ravilious. Its essence is a lyrical simplicity in which the subject is accurately summarized but the colour and touch of the medium are allowed a stronger role. There is the same feeling as before the war for grouped architecture, but a new breadth in the treatment of its setting and a delight in the long brushstroke with which plants and branches are represented. To a degree the influence of Paul Nash, though never lost, seems to be replaced by that of his brother John, a close friend. Looking through the large number of accomplished and poetic watercolours she made, it comes as a surprise to learn that she never regarded herself as a professional painter and that she had only one solo exhibition (at the New Grafton Gallery, Bond Street). Less than three months after this exhibition closed she died on 22 November 1979.

The principal work of Helen Binyon's last years was this memoir of

Eric Ravilious. It is marked by the same qualities of clarity, perceptive and often amusing observation and admiration in any art for the highest standards, which characterized her own fastidious work as artist and teacher. A perfectionist, she held back more from making her own achievements known than one feels her work justifies. It is therefore a source of satisfaction that she lived to complete this memoir. Its concern with wood engraving and watercolour from inside each art complements her writings on puppetry. It enables those who did not know her to gain a more rounded impression of a gifted individual who was not only important in the life of Eric Ravilious but made a valuable contribution in her own right to the art of her time.

In the preparation of this introduction I have been greatly helped by many of the family and friends of both Eric Ravilious and Helen Binyon, and I should like to add my thanks to those which were expressed earlier in the book.

1 'The Nautical Style', *Architectural Review*, January 1938.

2 J. M. Richards, *Memoirs of an Unjust Fella*, Weidenfeld and Nicolson, 1980, page 95; J. M. Richards was also the author of the text of *High Street*.

3 Though in the present book John Lake is quoted writing that even before he went to the Royal College Ravilious 'always seemed to be slightly somewhere else, as if he lived a private life which did not completely coincide with material existence. This made me feel a very earthy person when in his company'.

4 It should be noted that at approximately the same time as Palmer's etchings were making a strong impact on the young Graham Sutherland, Ravilious and Bawden, also students, made a 'pilgrimage' to Palmer's Shoreham.

5 'Sculpture in the Open Air', a talk by Moore recorded for the British Council, 1955, and published in Philip James, ed., *Henry Moore on Sculpture*, Macdonald, 1966, pages 97–109.

6 Information from *Dictionary of National Biography*.

7 Helen Binyon, *Puppetry Today*, Studio Vista, 1966, pages 13–14.

8 Two of the works given were 'The Seven Ages of Man' and 'Old Spain'; the words of both are published in Montagu Slater, *Peter Grimes and other poems*, The Bodley Head, 1946, pages 58–75 (in performance a simplified version of 'The Seven Ages of Man' was used). In 'Britten in the Theatre', in *Tempo* No. 107, December 1973, Eric Walter White states that the music was for singer, clarinet, violin, piano and celesta but that the manuscript scores disappeared in the war. Mrs Higgens (Margaret Binyon) and Sir Lennox Berkeley both recall that each composer wrote the music for a separate work. Mrs Higgens believes that Britten's was for 'Old Spain', including wailing music for the black-clad women.

Chapter 1

One September morning in 1922, a group of young men and women were waiting outside the door of the principal's room in the Royal College of Art. We were the new students arriving for our first day, and were being summoned, one by one, to an interview with the principal, William Rothenstein. We were to be assigned to one of the four schools – Painting, Design, Sculpture or Architecture – whose professors were also present. The last student to appear was Edward Bawden who came from Braintree in Essex. At a rather confusing interview with Rothenstein, who mistook him for someone else, it was decided that Bawden would study book illustration in the School of Design. From Rothenstein's office he found his way to the students' common room and, going into the canteen, he noticed a group of new students sitting at a table and listening to one of their number, a good-looking young man, whose large dark eyes lit up with enthusiasm as he talked animatedly about Sussex. This was Eric Ravilious; Bawden felt attracted to him at once, and joined the group. He found that Ravilious had also been assigned to the Design School to take his diploma in book illustration, and thus began a friendship that was to be of great importance to the artistic development of each of them.

Eric Ravilious was talking about Sussex because he had come from there the day before; his home was at Eastbourne, where he had spent nearly all his life. He was born in Acton, where his father had a draper's shop, and he was the youngest of four children. The eldest, a girl called Catherine, had died in infancy; then came Frank, born in 1892, Evelyn, born in 1896, and seven years later, on 22 July 1903, Eric William.

The name Ravilious comes from the French and was probably the name (possibly in a corrupted form) of a Huguenot refugee. (There are names like Revel, Revelion, Revalier, Rivalin, Revelliod, in the Returns Aliens in London of 1593 and in the Kent Records of 1650.) At any rate Eric's grandfather, James, had owned a tailoring business in Acton: Frank, Eric's father, was one of the youngest of seven or so children.

A family photograph, taken in Acton before Eric was born, shows a group carefully composed by the photographer, with Mrs Ravilious standing over her family. Perched on a high stool in front of her is a fair, white-frocked little girl, Evelyn; and the boy Frank sits between her and his father. No one is smiling – Mr Ravilious looks rather solemn, but his eyes are bright. It is a little difficult to recognize in him the impulsive and quick-tempered – even sometimes frightening – parent described by his descendants, but easier to imagine him in his old age, ill in hospital, and talking ecstatically to his visitor about his glorious visions of heaven.

He was a remarkable character, single-minded in his passion for his own personal version of Christianity and his own interpretations of Biblical prophecies. These were much more real to him than the problems of everyday life, and there were many financial crises during Eric's boyhood.

Eric's mother was Emma Ford, the daughter of a coachman living in Kingsbridge in Devon. Eric was devoted to her – indeed everyone seems to have loved her – and it was she who was the stabilizing influence in the household.

Eric's brother's wife described her parents-in-law in these words:

I would say that Frank's father was the unpractical, impulsive one, rather hasty in judgement and inclined to be over optimistic, and the family fortunes fluctuated considerably at different times; very penitent when he felt he had done wrong, and anxious in an almost child-like way to make amends. Mother was a much more serene character, a very good manager, slow to make up her mind and then difficult to move, always kindly and helpful, and devoted to her family, while acknowledging their failings.

Mrs Ravilious's other daughter-in-law, Eric's wife Tirzah, believed that Eric inherited his originality and ability as a craftsman from his father, while from his charming Devonshire mother came his integrity and his generosity.

When the draper's shop in Acton failed, the family moved to Eastbourne, where the Raviliouses had an antique shop. There Eric spent a happy childhood; he seems to have been able to abstract himself in spirit from the emotional pressures coming from his father's religious obsessions and from the intermittent difficulties about money – a talent that was noticed by his companions in later life.

And what could be more delightful for a child than the environment of a family shop? As a schoolboy, he had been delighted to discover *The History of Mr Polly* by H. G. Wells, and had a fellow feeling for this other boy whose father had a shop (although his favourite book, then and all his life, was *Huckleberry Finn*). His keen eye for discovering amusing or beautiful objects must have developed during his childhood, and it was in the shop that he first came across examples of the English Watercolour School.

The Ravilious family before Eric was born. **From left to right** *Frank Ravilious, Emma Ravilious, Frank and Evelyn.*

The first school that Eric was sent to was a little church school at Willingdon, on the outskirts of Eastbourne. In 1914, when he was eleven, he went on to the Eastbourne Grammar School, where he was very popular with staff and pupils alike, being of a sunny disposition and full of fun. He was keen on sport, and this love of games remained with him all his life; he enjoyed ball games of every kind – tennis, billiards, cricket – pub games like darts and shove-halfpenny, and paper games like 'Heads, bodies and legs', although he did not care for card games or crossword puzzles.

His artistic talent was also beginning to manifest itself. After he had embarked on his career as an artist and designer Eric found it very useful to have 'scrap books' of all the odds and ends that he felt might be worth keeping: first try-outs of designs and patterns, cuttings from newspapers, photographs, odd bits of information, working notes, tracings for engravings, anything that might be useful as a possible reference, germs of ideas, or just records. These were stuck, in no particular order, in large, fat books. In a collection of his childhood drawings is one dated 22 October 1914, when he was eleven years old and had just gone to the grammar school. It is a pencil drawing of an egg in an egg cup, which already shows the delicacy and clarity which were to be so characteristic of his work as an artist. The number 8, written so unfeelingly in red chalk near to the drawing, is presumably a mark from his teacher.

There are some drawings in pencil and in pen-and-ink, and some watercolours, dated September 1916 when he was thirteen. One of the watercolours is of Sissinghurst Castle, in which he has obviously enjoyed the patterns of the red bricks. It shows the keep with the two towers, each with its weather-vane sensitively noted. On the opposite page the painting is of a cottage with an adjacent oast-house, also of red brick. The colour scheme is very much the same as that of the Sissinghurst painting, the light red of the bricks against the strong green of a hedge in front and trees at the side. But the bold linear patterns of the upper storey of the half-timbered cottage may have been one of his reasons for choosing this subject.

Of the other drawings, mostly of farm buildings, the most interesting is a pencil drawing of one end of a tall building, set in an orchard and seen behind a fence and a five-barred gate. It is the treatment of the grove of apple trees that is interesting, instead of a generalization of the leafiness

Eric standing between his brother Frank and his sister Evelyn.

Eric's egg, drawn when he was 11.

– usually a baffling subject for a beginner – there is a real searching for the forms of growth, as well as their patterns, and they have been drawn with great delicacy, though naturally with the uncertain technique of a schoolboy.

In December 1919 he went in for the Cambridge Senior Local Examination, which he passed with distinction in drawing, and he was awarded a scholarship to the Eastbourne School of Art, where he was to work for the next three years.

The students were expected to work hard. A copy of the timetable for Eric's first term still exists. There were classes every morning, including Saturday, every afternoon except Saturday, and evening classes on Tuesdays and Fridays; the different subjects to be studied were still life, elementary design, pen drawing, lettering, nature study, antique, composition, life, and three classes for object drawing.

At the School of Art he made friends and with two other students, John Lake and Donald Towner, and they became his special companions. John Lake wrote for me the following account of the school and staff and of their time there:

I suppose that the Eastbourne School of Art was somehow functioning during the First World War. I first attended as an evening student in 1919. Ravilious and Towner – we never used Christian names in those days – were there as full-time students when I arrived. A. F. Reeve-Fowkes, the Principal, had not yet been demobilized, and the school was run by Miss Wood, a charming, gentle creature, assisted by A. B. Higgs, a meticulous pen-and-ink draughtsman, wood engraver and printer.

From the first Ravilious had an extraordinary, almost Pan-like charm and was a shy but very amusing person who from time to time came up with some most unexpected remarks. He and I played tennis together outside school hours and were usually partnered by the two Ryder girls whose father owned one of the three good bookshops in the town. . . . It was the originality of both Towner, and Ravilious in particular, which impressed me. . . . I always particularly admired and indeed was envious of Eric's *hands* and I can see them now in my mind's eye. The delicate, long, sensitive, spatulate fingers were something that I envied and did not myself possess. I also remember that Eric had charmingly amusing and original ideas about fancy dress, and this reminds me of a quality of which you must have been aware: that he always seemed to be slightly somewhere else, as if he lived a private life which did not completely coincide with material existence. This made me feel a very earthy person when in his company.

Towner, in those days, was an eccentric character, who as a young student was influenced by the early English water-colour painters. He liked singing Elizabethan songs, wore his hair long and was the most romantic-looking of the students. Both Towner and Ravilious left Eastbourne to go to the Royal College a year before I did, but before they went we all were elected members of the Brighton Arts Club and I seem to remember that we all sold our small paintings reasonably well.

In their last year Towner and Ravilious went into Brighton for life-drawing classes; possibly because there were no nude models at Eastbourne then. There was no mention of painting on that first timetable but, of course, they soon worked a lot in both oils and watercolours and in the summer terms went out to sketch in the countryside. At the end of one summer term, the three friends – Lake, Towner and Ravilious – organized a sketching holiday. 'We started', writes Lake,

in the general direction of my home in Hampshire. Before setting out from Eastbourne we made a pact, to which we kept, that we would never pay for a night's lodging. The first night we slept out on the Downs near Littlington; it was an unusually cold one. Ravilious had brought sensible clothes, but I had to lend some of mine to Towner who had to go home for more early the next morning, whilst Ravilious and I were having breakfast. We had various adventures on that long trip. Once we had a young female audience whilst we were drying after nude bathing at Amberly, at another the young children of our host stole various articles of clothing from the garage which was our bed-room, so that when we woke we had to chase them round the garden dressed in whatever they had chosen to leave us.

Towner remembers his annoyance at being woken sometimes in the night by Ravilious's loud laughter in his sleep – so entertaining were his dreams. All through his life Eric had fascinating dreams, which he would sometimes recount.

At Amberley, where we stayed for some time, and did quite a lot of work, we were invited to a small dance given by a family called Statton, who had at least two rather beautiful daughters, as well as a son. We arrived in the only clothes we had and wearing hob-nailed boots. The studio was illuminated by candles stuck in Chinese lanterns suspended from the ceiling. During the course of the evening the candles began to burn out with the danger of setting fire to the paper lanterns. Eric seized a billiard cue and potted them from below, which proved quite effective but covered everyone with candle grease. When we got as far as Bosham, the weather broke at last, so our weeks' long expedition ended there.

I suppose that what I remember best of all about those far-off years was the feeling of great freedom and happiness – this period in our lives, when we were starting to educate ourselves, instead of being educated, gave us an extraordinary sense of wonder and excitement.

The Eastbourne School of Art awarded one scholarship a year to the Royal College of Art, an exceptionally meagre one of £60 a year. In the examination for it, Ravilious came second; the student who came first decided at the last moment that her vocation was really to be a missionary, so she gave up the scholarship and it was passed on to Ravilious.

There was a day's test of life-drawing to be taken at the college itself. When Ravilious and Towner arrived at the college they were taken to a studio where the model, a man, was waiting to pose. There was only one other student, from another school, taking the test. They were provided with paper on imperial-sized drawing boards. This was twice as large a size as Towner and Ravilious were used to, but they bravely filled their page. The other student, whose name, it appeared, was Edward Burra, spent the day making a very beautiful study, in the middle of his page, of one of the model's eyes. Towner and Burra were accepted by the college as well, and all three arrived there for the first day of the autumn term of 1922.

Donald Towner in the 1920s.

Chapter 2

In the England of the early 1920s the Slade School enjoyed the highest reputation of the art schools, being famous for the teaching of Henry Tonks and Wilson Steer. Few people in the London art world could have told you anything about the Royal College of Art, or even where it was.

It had been the idea of the Prince Consort that a new Museum of Science and Art should be built in South Kensington, and contain collections from three sources: from the Great Exhibition of 1851; the Museum of Manufactures, established by the Department of Science and Art in 1852, and from the Government School of Design. The new museum was opened in 1857, but the collections grew, and new ones were donated, so that by 1891 additional building was necessary. The foundation stone of this new extension was laid by Queen Victoria in 1899, who directed that its name should be the Victoria and Albert Museum. It was opened by Edward VII in 1909, the scientific part of the collection having been taken off to form the new Science Museum.

The Government School of Design was still in its first home in the original part of the building, but was now called the Royal College of Art. Its chief function was to produce teachers for the provincial art schools, as well as designers for industry. In 1910 a government committee had been set up to inquire into the scope of the Royal College of Art, but nothing seems to have come of it until after the First World War. In 1919 the Prime Minister, Lloyd George, appointed a new president of the Board of Education, H. A. L. Fisher, who decided that, as the chief Government School of Art, the prestige of the Royal College must be raised, and that a change of policy was desirable. He asked William Rothenstein to be the new principal and to undertake this mission.

Herbert Fisher had first met Rothenstein in Paris in the 1890s, where the young history don from New College was attending lectures at the Sorbonne and the artist – then seventeen and fresh from the Slade School – was studying at Julian's Academy. Rothenstein blossomed in the artistic milieu, with the encouragement of many painters, poets and writers – Degas, Whistler, Camille Pissarro, Conder, Bonnard, Vuillard, Max Beerbohm, Verlaine and Mallarmé – of most of whom he drew portraits. Fisher became Vice-Chancellor of Sheffield University in 1917 and invited Rothenstein to give a series of annual lectures. He clearly recognized Rothenstein's qualities not only as a painter, but also as a witty speaker with a talent for expressing his ideas.

Rothenstein's acceptance of the new appointment to the Royal College raised a storm of protest in the National Society of Art Masters. Here was a plum job being given to an unqualified teacher and a painter with no experience of the crafts: no wonder they were furious. But they had to accept it, and by the autumn of 1922 Rothenstein had already begun to make the changes he felt to be necessary. It was an interesting moment

The Royal College of Art.
Above, left *Diploma
Day, 1923.* **From left to
right** *Miss Potts of the
Engraving School,
Professors William
Rothenstein, Robert
Anning Bell and Frank
Short.* **Above right** *In
the Common Room –
Cecilia Dunbar Kilburn,
Eric Ravilious, Anthony
Betts.*

for the eighteen-year-old Ravilious to be starting his career as a student.

Although on that first morning all the new students had been told to which of the four Schools they would belong, they found that for their first term they were all to work in the School of Architecture for an introductory course under Professor Beresford Pite. That was to be for four days a week, from half-past nine in the morning to half-past three in the afternoon, and then drawing classes from four to six in the evening. There were drawing classes on Wednesday mornings, too, but the afternoon was free, with opportunities for playing hockey, football or cricket for those students who wanted to do so. Ravilious was one of these, but not his new friend Bawden.

The life-drawing classes were primarily for painting and sculpture students. Design students might be started on plant drawing; some would be promoted to draw plaster casts from the antique, and finally allowed to draw from a model. Ravilious had already done much more life-drawing than most of the design students, and was admitted to the life-classes from the beginning. In fact when, later on, some students' life-drawings, of varying styles, were chosen by staff to be pinned up on a wall to inspire the rest of us, I remember noticing a sensitive, rather tentative pencil drawing, signed with the name Ravilious.

There were four or five teachers with rather confusingly different advice about drawing to give the new students. In the women's life-class, for instance, we would have started drawings when the door would open and in would come the principal – a short, slight figure, wearing very emphatic horn-rimmed glasses. Those students who had taken his advice to buy plumb lines for themselves now held them out, and tried to use them to test the perpendiculars in their drawings. Rothenstein's ideal was the pencil drawing of Ingres. He would go round the class, criticizing, advising, and perhaps sharpening the blunt pencil a student was trying to draw with, and then would go out. A little later, the door would open again; heads would turn to see who it was this time. A larger, clumsier man would stand waiting in the doorway; a thick dark fringe of hair covered the top of his face, while the lower part was obscured by his hand, the fingernails of which he was biting. The weaker students felt a little shiver of fear. It was Leon Underwood, the exponent of 'Form', of cylinder and section; drawings would darken, line was out, shading was all important.

Underwood, one of Rothenstein's new appointments, was a great source of inspiration to some of the painting and sculpture students, and ran special classes at his own home later in the evenings, for a chosen group of students which at this time included Henry Moore, Raymond Coxon, Barbara Hepworth and Enid Marx.

The College's Common Room was a remarkable institution, financed and run entirely and very efficiently by student committees. The food was simple but quite good, and in London art-student circles reputedly the cheapest, yet there were sometimes profits from it to help finance the students' magazine. Committee members took it in turn to help hand out the food from a counter, and then would find their way to one of the small tables arranged up one half of the long room. There was one larger table which was known as the 'Leeds table' because the students who sat there, who seemed more lively and confident, were mostly from the Leeds School of Art. Most of the men had been in the First World War, and so were a little older than the other students, and they were determined to make the most of their time.

And then the girls wore such charming clothes. In the early 1920s there was only one fashionable colour – it was called 'beige' and was a pinkish café-au-lait. Ordinary girls wore skimpy straight and knee-length dresses of this universal colour, with very low waists, and front and back as flat as possible. Hair was cut very short, under cloche hats pulled right down over it. But the more dashing art-students would have none of this; they chose beautiful strong colours – scarlet, lemon, magenta, black – and in the little Common-Room sewing-room they made themselves long full skirts and bodices which emphasized their waists and their feminine curves. A wide-brimmed black felt hat might be worn with a dark cloak, and with sandals if possible.

Everyone was hard up, and a few painfully so; Ravilious might have been one of these, if his mother had not helped him by sending him a little money when she could. Common Room life had an important place in college education. Most students lived in lodgings, cheap bed-sitting rooms in Fulham or Earl's Court. Ravilious found himself a bed-sitting room of 'comical disagreeableness', but was soon able to move to other lodgings nearer to Edward Bawden and another student called Douglas Percy Bliss, whom Bawden had got to know in the Architecture School. These three found each other's company immensely stimulating – Bliss, already a graduate of Edinburgh University, with a degree in English, was a student in the Painting School. His literary explorations and discoveries were now shared with his two friends, and the three of them talked about books all the time.

This is how Bliss described 'Rav', as his friends at college called him:

He was a delightful companion, cheerful, good-natured, intelligent and prepossessing in appearance. He was not robust physically, nor was he delicate. He could play a good game of tennis, but had no surplus energy. He tired easily and suffered often from what he called 'a thick head' – I never saw him depressed. Even when he fell in love – and that was frequent – he was never submerged by disappointment. Cheerfulness kept creeping in. . . .

Some students at the R.C.A. worked far too hard. They never found time to relax. But E.R. spent hours in the Students' Common Room with the prettier kind of girl and never missed a dance. But he was not idle. He was educating himself, finding in the indigestible superabundance of the great city's art the particular nourishment he needed. He was fastidious and assimilative, culling his fruits from any bough, trying out conventions from Gothic tapestries, Elizabethan painted-cloths, the wood-cuts of Incunabula, or Persian miniatures. He had exquisite taste and sifted with the skill of an anthologist the rare things that could help him in his work. In the great dish of Art confronting us in South Kensington, like Mrs Todgers, he 'dodged about among the tender pieces with a fork'. Ravilious went his own way, rather like a sleep-walker, but with a sure step and an unswerving instinct for style.

And he was usually whistling in that special way he had, which his friends remember so well, and have described as 'better than a nightingale'. Cecilia Dunbar Kilburn has written of 'that enchanting way he had of whistling; it sounded as though he whistled in thirds, but perhaps it was such a rapid trill it seemed like two notes at the same time.'

Edward Bawden was certainly one of the students described by Bliss as working far too hard. Except with his intimate friends he was shy and unsociable. As Bliss wrote about him once, 'girls scared him and he hated all hale and hearty fellows. He stood a little outside life. He saw it like a foreigner at a cricket-match, marvelling at its madness.'

Bawden and Ravilious were drawn together by their special sense of humour. Bawden's was the more sardonic, but they both had a wonderfully keen eye for any oddity or absurdity in their surroundings. Bawden was much less easy-going than the other two, and could infuriate as well as delight them, but they were inseparable companions, except in official classes, when Bliss would be working in the painting studios, Bawden and Ravilious in the design room.

After the first term of architecture, the new design students were able to settle down to work at their chosen subjects. Bawden and Ravilious chose two places next to each other in the front right-hand corner of the design room, where they could be undisturbed by the sight of their fellow students. The professor of design was Robert Anning Bell, but it was his last year. His students did not see much of him, but he was encouraging to the two friends, and took them to hear Arthur Rackham talking to the Art-Workers Guild about book illustration, and to a Royal Academy Club dinner.

E. W. Tristram, who was Anning Bell's assistant, and succeeded him as professor the following year, was more accessible. He looked rather like a figure in one of the medieval wall paintings on which he was an authority: very thin and stiff and straight, with a narrow bony face and an unchanging expression. He talked very little, but he was helpful, and prodded the students in some of the right directions: this freedom suited Bawden and Ravilious well.

One of Rothenstein's first moves at the college was to persuade the Board of Education to allow him to employ part-time artists as well as full-time teachers. The most imaginative of these appointments was that of Paul Nash to teach once a week in the Design School.

Some years earlier, before the war, Rothenstein had been asked to give a criticism of the students' compositions at Bolt Court (now the London School of Printing) and had singled out one drawing as having exceptional promise; it was by the young Paul Nash, and since that time Rothenstein had kept in touch with him. Of course by the time he was invited to the college, Nash had made his reputation with his very impressive war paintings, and with several one-man exhibitions.

Ravilious and Bawden had both worked in watercolours before they went to the college, but in London, in the Victoria and Albert Museum Print Room and in other galleries, they were able to see paintings by the artists they particularly admired – William Alexander, J. R. Cozens, Thomas Girtin, J. S. Cotman, and particularly Francis Towne and Samuel Palmer, whose work was almost unknown at the time. So excited were they by an exhibition of Palmers that the two students, together with Bliss, made a pilgrimage to Shoreham where Samuel Palmer had worked.

Ravilious and Bawden had been captivated by the 'breath-taking freshness' of the latest London shows of watercolour paintings by Paul Nash and his brother, John, so their new tutor's appearance one morning in the design room was an important event. Paul Nash was tallish, with a hint of plumpness, and had very thick shining black hair, smoothly brushed back from his brown-skinned face, with blue eyes, curving nose and red lips. He wore a bow tie and a dark suit and looked almost too smart for an artist. He would wander down the long room, looking carefully at what the students had to show him; he was witty and jokey and often encouraging, or he might say 'this is just what we want to get away from'. He was particularly helpful with watercolours, demonstrating ways of using the medium, trying out colours with a starved as well as a full brush, or washing one transparent colour over a ground of another.

Paul Nash had been making some beautiful wood engravings at this time, and was interested in Ravilious's first experiments in this craft, helping him later with introductions to publishers. Nash was experimenting in various other directions; for instance, he had designed the sets and costumes for a curious half play, half ballet written by Sir James Barrie for the dancer Karsavina, and performed at the Coliseum. In those days the Diaghilev Ballet Company used to come for a season to the Coliseum, giving a different ballet at each performance, as one of the turns in a regular music hall programme. Ravilious was not himself a fan of the Russian ballet. His enthusiasm at that time was for a revival of Nigel Playfair's 1920 production of *The Beggar's Opera* at the Lyric

*Model for Claud Lovat Fraser's set for Peachum's House, Act I, **The Beggar's Opera** 1921. Theatre Museum, Victoria & Albert Museum*

Theatre, Hammersmith. The designer was Claud Lovat Fraser, whose use of brilliant primary colours had shocked and delighted London audiences. The music was lovely, and Ravilious sang or whistled the old tunes happily and endlessly.

Paul Nash had made friends with Lovat Fraser not long before his sudden death in 1921. As well as sharing a lively interest in theatre design, the two artists had new ideas about decorations for the printed page. They had each, for instance, made designs for Harold Munro's *Broadsheets*, published from the Poetry Bookshop in Bloomsbury – Lovat Fraser had decorated four rhyme sheets and three songs from *The Beggar's Opera*, Paul Nash a poem by Ezra Pound, John Nash one by Walt Whitman. Bawden, Bliss and Ravilious were enchanted with the *Broadsheets* when they first came across them in the Victoria and Albert Museum Library, and Bawden bought some to pin round his room.

At this time Ravilious was as much interested in mural painting as in book illustration. Edward Bawden had this to say of him during this period at the college:

> To take Dip – the R.C.A. Diploma – needed three years but Eric had to take it in two as the grant from Eastbourne was insufficient for the full course. He picked on mural decoration as his examination subject. As then taught, mural dec, as it was affectionately called, meant the preparation of gesso panels, using egg tempera, grinding earth colour, and playing about with gold leaf, all simple enough to do but made more tricky if one followed Cennino Cennini's ancient recipes; but to follow them, though it was counted a sign of merit, seldom proved to be a surefire guide to success – Eric, who was off-hand and casual, ignored Cennini, he failed to slake whiting or grind gritty colour or touch an egg. Yet the Boy, as we called him, came out a winner – when the dip screens were removed it was seen that he had used bought gesso powder and ordinary colour, moreover he had slapped up a big gay painting that really had some pretensions to being a mural. The Boy passed dip with distinction and was awarded the Design School Travelling Scholarship.

Travelling scholars invariably went to Italy; when Henry Moore won the Sculpture School scholarship that same year, he asked the new registrar, Hubert Wellington, if instead of going to Italy, he could go to Berlin or Paris to study Egyptian sculpture, in which he was much more interested than in Renaissance sculpture. But this was impossible, he was told, as the money was kept waiting for the scholars in Florence, Rome or Venice and had to be claimed there. So to Florence he went, and managed to find some of the sustenance he wanted from Giotto, Masaccio, Michelangelo, and some primitive carvings, and to stay two or three weeks in Paris on the way back. But though excited by what he had seen, he said he felt that he had aesthetic indigestion when he got home, and considered that it took him four months to recover his own direction.

Ravilious seems to have felt baffled and unsure of himself on this his first visit abroad, and unwilling to make the regulation copies of Italian paintings expected of travelling scholars. He stayed most of the time in Florence – with brief visits to San Gimignano, Siena, and Volterra – and enjoyed most of all going for long walks by himself along the banks of the Arno, miles into the countryside. Three little wood engravings were sent home as evidence of what he had seen there. Like Moore, he found that the superabundance of art all round him stifled the wish to do his own work, though later when he was back in England, and had left the college, he made admirable use of what he had learnt in Italy.

There were other students from the college in Florence at the same time, as well as Henry Moore: Norman Dawson from the Painting School and Edna Ginesi and Robert Lyon, who had just won the Prix de Rome. (Thus was one of Rothenstein's ambitions for the college achieved, the Prix de Rome competition being open to students from all the art schools). On the strength of his prize, Bob Lyon had just married (not officially allowed at that time) and he and his charming wife, Mabel, had taken half a flat in Florence, to which the other college students often went in the evenings, to meet and exchange news of their day's activities; or they might go to a nearby restaurant after the regular meal, which they could not afford, to have coffee and fruit and to dance to the music of violins. On Sundays the Lyons sometimes took Ravilious for a picnic, exploring the countryside around Florence. They stopped once at an inn, where the proprietor asked them about themselves, and became flatteringly attentive when told about the Prix de Rome. They felt privileged to be in a country where art was held in such respect. But this proved to be an illusion; the inn-keeper thought it was the Rome bicycle race that Lyon had won.

Italy at this time was in a state of political unrest. The signs were ominous; that summer the poet Matteotti had been killed by Fascists outside the British School in Rome, and his body thrown into the Tiber at the Porta del Popolo. In Florence, the Lyons would occasionally hear shots in the street, and their landlady would rush up to their room, crying, 'Keep away from the window.' Mabel Lyon remembers standing one day with Ravilious at the bridge of Santa Trinita, while a large detachment of Mussolini's Blackshirts tramped endlessly across the bridge. The people in the road watched in silence; there was a chill of fear in the air. Mabel felt this, but perhaps not Ravilious. He was not at all interested in politics.

Robert and Mabel Lyon stayed in Italy, soon going on to Rome, but all the others came home, laden with Alinari photographs of works of art. Henry Moore told his friends the Coxons, of the Painting School,

Travelling Scholars from the R.C.A. in Florence: Robert Lyon, Eric Ravilious, Henry Moore; **seated in front** *Mrs Robert Lyon and Norman Dawson.*

31

that he had got to know a design student called Ravilious, whose company he had much enjoyed; this was a surprising statement, for the painting and sculpture students felt themselves to be pursuing aims so much more serious and elevated than those of the design students that there was little contact between them at college.

Another student, Vivian Pitchforth, remembers that his first knowledge and appreciation of Rav's work started with the Students Sketch Club Exhibition, always held after the summer holidays. In his view, 'these shows always separated the sheep from the goats'. He took the quality and number of exhibits from each student as evidence as to which of them promised to be good artists of the future. At one of these exhibitions he had specially noticed the 'Bawden-Rav watercolours'; other students whose work he had found promising were Barnett Freedman, Enid Marx and Albert Houthuesen. These three were all painting students, but in a few years' time, Barnett Freedman in lithography, and Enid Marx in textiles, had in fact made names for themselves as designers.

One of Rothenstein's important contributions to the college was the sharing with his students of his friendships with many of the most gifted men of his generation. He would often bring his distinguished sitters over to the Common Room to meet the students. Vivian Pitchforth remembers the visit of Rabindranath Tagore, 'tall and stately in his Indian robes, with a long white beard and high-pitched voice and the Indian students kissing his feet'; Lawrence of Arabia 'very quiet', and G. K. Chesterton, 'rather grubby in a large black hat and cape'.

There would also be evenings at the Rothenstein's house in Airlie Gardens, to which groups of students would be invited; there, as mentioned in his book *Men and Memories*, they might have met Gordon Craig or James Stephens, Ralph Hodgson or Arnold Bennett. Once Ravilious was excited to find himself in the presence of Max Beerbohm whose drawings he particularly liked, but Max was carried off by Lady Cunard before there was a possibility of speaking to him – even if the Boy could have overcome his shyness enough to do so. However, except for those he saw much of – and they were the most gifted and the most intelligent – the students on the whole did not appreciate Rothenstein. They felt he represented something alien and antiquated, and some were dull enough to mock at his allusions to what he had heard Degas saying thirty years before. In his own student days Rothenstein had written 'the very young are suspicious of artists who frequent fashionable circles'. Many of his own students now felt exactly the same way about him.

When Ravilious got back to England and the college, he found himself caught up in the new enthusiasm for wood engraving, which Bliss also shared. Some of their earliest experiments had been printed in the R.C.A. students' magazine, of which Bliss took on the editorship in his second year. He was cautious to begin with, using the same handsome but staid design for the cover as had his predecessors, but for the third number of June 1925 and with the help of his two friends, he decided to break new ground. This new spirit was proclaimed by the magazine's new name of *Gallimaufry*, drawn on a bold new cover designed by Ravilious. Inside there were also two wood engravings by him; one of them, the frontispiece, was larger than any he had done before, and more varied in technique. In fact he was just beginning to find his own style.

In his editorial, Bliss commends the magazine to its readers, writing, 'We have tried to give you something cheerier, with clearer type, more

Eric Ravilious's cover design for **Gallimaufry** *June 1925.*

stimulating designs and a touch of colour, hand-applied by the Committee for love of you all.'

The *Gallimaufry* had some success; the Keeper of Prints and Drawings at the British Museum, Campbell Dodgson, bought several copies, exhibiting two in the print room, and giving one to the Bibliothéque Nationale in Paris. Francis Meynell, who had recently founded the Nonesuch Press, was interested in the method of adding colour, and persuaded Bliss to help him with the hand colouring of one of the Nonesuch books. Even while they were still at college, the three students had been getting some professional work, especially Bawden. But it was Bliss who was the first to have a book published, in his third year at college. This was *Border Ballads*, a selection made by him, and illustrated with wood engravings.

But college days were coming to an end – Bawden was awarded that year's Travelling Scholarship in Design, and in London, Ravilious and Bliss moved from their bed-sitters to share a more spacious studio in Redcliffe Road. Before them, it had housed first Bob Lyon and then Ted Halliday, fellow students from the Painting School who had each in turn won the Prix de Rome and left for Italy.

There were a number of college friends living in studios on the same side of Redcliffe Road, and when Bawden got back from his travels, he found a nearby studio for himself, and the three friends continued to see much of each other.

Chapter 3

For the next year or two, Ravilious and Bliss had as near neighbours in Redcliffe Road several other college friends as well as Bawden. There was Phyllis Dodd, a beautiful blonde and a portrait painter, who later became engaged to Bliss; George Branson, nicknamed by them the 'Bombinator', and Cecilia Dunbar Kilburn, who had worked with Bliss, Bawden and Ravilious on *Gallimaufry*, and was now editing its successor, the *Mandrake*. There were others too, of course, but this was the group of next-door neighbours who encouraged each other and helped out when supplies of one kind or another ran out.

There are still in existence some of their letters to each other written at this time. There is one from Bawden to Ravilious asking about the choice of a book to illustrate. His publishers, Dent, had finally turned down his own idea of doing *The Knight of the Burning Pestle*, and sent him instead this list of possible books: Beckford's *Vathek*, Pattock's *Fighting Indians*, Poe's *Tales*, Swift's *Tale of a Tub*, or Sterne's *Sentimental Journey*. 'Please advise what to choose or to refuse', wrote Bawden to Ravilious. He described himself as 'encumbered with petty commercial jobs, business letters, and general money-grubbing'.

Or, in 1927, Ravilious wrote from Eastbourne to Cecilia Dunbar Kilburn:

> I stay at home now for such long periods, Bliss is as pleased when I go up as if I had been abroad, and so am I pleased really. His conversation simply can't be replaced, not by anyone here at least. It is dreadfully priggish to say so, but there aren't more than three people I've come across here in Eastbourne that I really like talking to; if they are informed on anything it is something like military fortifications, or the Book of Daniel, or perspective. . . . Aren't Bliss and Bawden going it just at present; publishers fall to them, Bliss says, at the rate of four a week. Bawden is overdoing it now I think, he will kill himself. . . Do you know anyone he could marry? Perhaps God will create a wife (from a rib) for such a diligent servant as Edward. He is quite as particular a case as Adam.

Bliss, at home in Edinburgh, and also missing his friends' conversation, wrote to Cecilia Dunbar Kilburn too: 'I'm working hard, eating heartily, motoring, smug and extroverted – there are no dead-beat, mocking humourous Boys, no muck-raking humble Bombinators, no dry Bawdens' . . . and congratulating her on her editing of the second number of *Mandrake*, he asked her – 'why not become the first lady typographer? There was, circa 1490 a certain Yolande Bonhomme who carried on the work of her dead husband, Jacques Kerver and produced lovely Horae faultlessly struck off on vellum; but I know of no other lady-printer of eminence.'

There are letters from Cecilia Dunbar Kilburn to Rav; one from India, where she had spent the winter of 1927–28, with ecstatic descriptions of visiting Ipoh, Penang, Tampin, Malacca, Singapore, Rangoon, Mandalay, and up the Irawaddy River to within thirty miles of the Chinese frontier. Professor Rothenstein had given her many introductions to Indian friends of his, and she came home with a commission to sculpt a portrait-bust of a Rajah. He also wanted to have a bookplate made for himself, a job she passed on to Ravilious, who was, by now, an accomplished wood engraver.

In November 1925, soon after Ravilious had left the college, the Society of Wood Engravers had been holding its sixth annual exhibition at the Redfern Gallery in Bond Street. At a meeting of its members a month before, Eric Ravilious had been proposed for membership by Paul Nash; other artists proposed at this meeting were David Jones, Charles Ginner, John Farleigh and Enid Marx. They were all accepted.

The Society of Wood Engravers had been founded in 1920, by Robert Gibbings with the help of Noel Rooke. Its object was to set a standard for the craft, and to make it known by holding exhibitions. Other founder members were Lucien Pissarro of the Eragny Press, Gordon Craig, Eric Gill, Paul and John Nash, Philip Hagreen and Sidney Lee. Ethelbert White, Gwendolen Raverat, and Margaret Pilkington were elected very soon after, and Margaret Pilkington took on the secretaryship of the society, giving devoted service for many years.

At the beginning there had been disagreements – Gordon Craig resigned almost at once, and later a group with Leon Underwood, Blair Hughes-Stanton and Gertrude Hermes split off to form the English Wood-Engraving Society, and exhibit at another gallery.

Robert Gibbings had lately taken over the Golden Cockerel Press, which had been founded as a Writers' Co-operative by Hal Taylor. The first idea had been that a group of, as yet, unknown authors would share all the work of production – type-setting and printing, as well as writing the books; profits from sales would then also be shared. After enormous difficulties some books appeared, but except from one by A. E. Coppard, there were no profits to divide. The Press had to give up its first scheme, and change to the safer one of the fine printing of books already out of copyright.

Just before the First World War, Robert Gibbings had been a student of Noel Rooke's class at the Central School. Gibbings joined up in 1914, fought in the Dardanelles, and survived to come back to work as an illustrator in London. In 1922 he had a letter from a firm he had never heard of, called the Golden Cockerel Press, asking him to engrave some illustrations for them and then, almost at once, he heard that the Press was about to close down, as the founder was dying of tuberculosis. Impulsively, Robert Gibbings decided to borrow the money and to buy the Golden Cockerel Press himself. In the next nine years his Press produced seventy-two books, forty-eight of them decorated with wood engravings. Many of these were his own; his chief collaborator was Eric Gill. These two artists were of a slightly earlier generation than Ravilious, and Gibbings was naturally on the look-out for new young engravers. So his meeting with Ravilious through the Society of Wood Engravers was of importance to them both, and in the next few years, Ravilious did some of his most ambitious engraved illustrations for the Golden Cockerel Press.

Before the war the most serious and interesting experiments in fine printing had been made by the private presses, in which all the press-work was done by hand, and each edition limited to a comparatively small number. Inspired by the ideals of the Arts and Crafts Movement, and started by William Morris and his Kelmscott Press, the Doves Press, the Ashendene Press, the Vale Press and the Eragny Press had all printed beautiful books. If they had illustrations or decorations, these would have been printed from wood blocks of the same height as the type, so that illustration and type could be printed together.

The craft of wood engraving had been marvellously developed by Thomas Bewick in the late eighteenth century, but by the middle of the nineteenth its practitioners, though immensely skilful, lacked his creative genius, and their work was used to reproduce the pen-and-ink or pencil drawings of professional book illustrators. This was at a time when all books were expected to have illustrations of some kind, but by the latter half of the nineteenth century, the cheaper and quicker photographic processes of reproduction were replacing the commercial engravers.

Noel Rooke, working at the turn of the century, became dissatisfied by the photographic reproductions of his book illustrations, and wanted a return to the traditional method of wood engraving. But, he decided, 'a wood-engraving would only have the quality of an original work of art, if it were designed by the artist, graver in hand, with incisions dictated by the medium itself, and not by the quite alien pen or pencil'. In fact the artist must be an engraver. This Rooke became, and as he taught illustration at the Central School of Arts and Crafts, he was eventually given permission to teach wood engraving. One of his first students was Robert Gibbings.

This idea was taken up by other artists and teachers. Professor Anning Bell at the Royal College, to whom Ravilious had sent one of his engravings, wrote to him:

I was very pleased and interested to get your wood-engravings. This new experimental movement in the white line is well worth working at, and you appreciate the beauty of a line which some of our rasher young men do not seem to do – they prefer lumps and appear to assault the helpless wood block with an axe.

Through the influence of Noel Rooke, his student Robert Gibbings and the Golden Cockerel Press, wood engraving became an important part of book design in the 1920s and 1930s.

The first publisher to ask Ravilious to do some wood engravings was Jonathan Cape; the book was *Desert*, by Martin Armstrong. It came out in 1926, and it exemplified some of the problems of printing wood engravings. Ravilious was very disappointed when he saw the first copy of *Desert*, and the way the finely cut parts of his engravings had lost definition in places; but it made him reconsider the way he used his different tools – graver, spitsticker and scorper – and gradually develop the craftsmanship to make engravings that could be printed satisfactorily in a modern press.

His next two books were commissioned by Robert Gibbings for the Golden Cockerel Press, for which he also engraved five or six prospectuses.

A Ballad upon a Wedding, the poem by Sir John Suckling, is a small book with eight half-page illustrations, some of an attractive narrow shape, with the sides keeping the straight edges of the block, but with the

*An illustration for **Desert,
A Legend** by Martin
Armstrong (Jonathan
Cape, 1926).*

design breaking into new shapes at top and bottom. This is particularly successful on the title page. The problem of the printing is not yet solved and some of the blacks are patchy. The book is printed on a hard hand-made paper, used for all these Golden Cockerel books.

In the same year, 1927, Ravilious also illustrated *The Twelve Moneths*, by the minor Elizabethan poet Nicholas Breton. On the left-hand pages are printed his Countryman's thoughts about each month, while on the opposite pages the calendar for each month is set out in a rectangle, with engravings above and below. These illustrate the happenings alluded to in the text, but in terms of the artist's own day rather than an Elizabethan's. The engravings are still too finely cut for the paper, but there are some delightful personal observations of the country; particularly the boy bird's-nesting, which illustrates April.

But Ravilious did not work only for private presses. In the years after the war one or two young printers had sought to apply some of the traditions and standards of the private presses to more commercial printing done in commercial printing houses. In 1922 a publishing society called 'The Fleuron' was started by Stanley Morison, Oliver Simon, Holbrook Jackson, Bernard Newdigate and Francis Meynell, 'with the aim of producing one book a year to demonstrate to collectors and to anyone else who was interested that books set by machine could be as beautiful as the

Above *A Ballad Upon A Wedding* by Sir John Suckling, with engravings by Eric Ravilious (The Golden Cockerel Press, 1927). **Below** *A detail from 'April' in* ***The Twelve Moneths*** *by Nicholas Breton, edited by Brian Rhys, with wood engravings by Eric Ravilious (The Golden Cockerel Press, 1927). 'Here, as in a green recess, sounds all the merry running freshness of a country brook, the praise of a perpetual English April.'*

books of the Hand Presses'. They started the *Fleuron* magazine, and under Stanley Morison's supervision the Monotype Corporation began a programme of type design and revival – starting with Monotype Garamond in 1922 – making good typefaces available to commercial printers.

In 1928 Ravilious was asked by Stanley Morison to make twelve wood engravings for an almanack for 1929, to be published by the Lanston Monotype Corporation. (The name Lanston was soon to be left out of its title.) There was to be an engraving for each month, connected with the signs of the zodiac. Each engraving shows a mythological figure floating or alighting in a Sussex landscape: for example, in the illustration for July, Andromeda is delicately climbing a ladder up against a haystack under a starry sky.

All the engravings show a new mastery of technique; there is much more variety in the range of greys, and in the use of stipplings and hatchings, and they are well-printed on a smooth machine-made paper.

In 1929 the Cresset Press published an edition of the Apocrypha, with a different artist engraving the illustration for each of the fourteen chapters or extracts. The edition was limited to 450 copies on mould-made paper and to 30 copies on handmade paper, and it was printed at the Curwen Press. Ravilious illustrated 'The Song of the Three Holy Children in the burning fiery furnace and the Angel of the Lord coming down into the Oven'. It is an impressive design, larger than any of his earlier engravings, with the three naked children welcoming the Angel who is on a larger scale than they are; the convention used for the fiery flames is very successful.

In this same year Ravilious's other published engravings included some in *The Woodcut*, an annual edited by Herbert Furst and published by the

‘The Box Room’. This wood engraving by Eric Ravilious only appeared in the Special Edition of **The Woodcut** Volume IV (The Fleuron, 1930), of which there were 75 copies, ‘70 for sale’.

‘Sagittarius’ – December – in **Almanack 1929**, one of twelve designs engraved on wood (Lanston Monotype Corporation).

Fleuron, and another large illustration of 'Doctor Faustus conjuring Mephistophilis' for the *Legion Book*.

But busy as Ravilious must have been with all this engraving, he was painting whenever he could, as were Bawden and Bliss, and they kept in touch with each other when they left London for country scenes.

Here is part of a letter from Bawden to Bliss:

Dear Bliss, herewith I open the summer correspondence – I am most inquisitive to know what there is to know, especially how you are getting along? How are you? How's Edinburgh? How's Gossop? How's Woodcuts and Cervantes? How's this? How's that? Please write and tell us all – Mind I rely on you to tell us everything.

I have had news of Rav, because I sent him a piece of Red Cow – In return he sent a Cookery Book in French with some cuts of highly ornamental dishes. He tries to incite me to design a new Cookery Book; for whom I wonder? He writes in his letter of giblets and entrails, and the transparent architecture of jellies – Oh! very good. How Le Corbusier would have pondered over the last suggestion and no doubt would have photographed a few jellies for his *Vers une Architecture* – Jellies, apart from scale, are not unlike Santa Sophia and the Mosquée Verte. But more form: fuller! richer! Le Corbusier often comes very near to Rav's remarks – For instance he says, speaking of plans – 'Mon édifice est comme une bulle de savon' – Why? because 'l'extérieur est le résultat d'une intérieur' – So let us think of jellies rising in ruby splendour, their heads capped by clustering domes; a centre dome mightier than the rest. . . .

By the next letter Ravilious has joined Bawden in Essex, and Bawden writes again to Bliss:

We have been biking about quite a lot together. The day the Boy arrived we biked out to a place five or six miles away, which I had been keeping in my eye for some time. It is a small village, with a fine church, in front of which stands a dark pond diapered over with ducks, and overshadowed by elms; the whole enclosed in a semi-private manner.

In fact it really was wholly private, and the owner, 'a tall flat-breasted woman', appeared, and after some scolding from her, and some argument from the artists, they were turned away.

Ravilious said we achieved a great moral victory by our calm and dignified politness.

But what I wanted to write to you about was not this but about the show. Howell in a letter to me mentions he would like our stuff by the second week in September. We think it is a bit early. If it could be put off – say for a month – What do you think? . . . We mustn't have a hotch-potch affair. We must march to Howell with victory gleaming in our eyes.

A. R. Howell was the owner of the little St George's Gallery in George Street, off Hanover Square, who was generous in encouraging young artists. He was interested in watercolour painting, and had shown the work of the young Paul and John Nash, and that of Ethelbert White. He was also ready to have exhibitions of wood engravings, unlike most of the other galleries at this time, and the break-away English Wood-En-

'Dr Faustus Conjuring Mephistopheles' from **The Legion Book** (printed by the Curwen Press, published by Cassells, 1929). Edited by Captain H. Cotton Minchin, the book was 'sold in aid of the British Legion by the wishes of His Majesty the King as a thank offering for his recovery.'

graving Society exhibited there. It was through his work as a wood engraver that Bliss had got to kow the gallery, and it was he who had persuaded Howell to launch his two friends and himself in a first show of paintings.

There was much correspondence between the three of them, about the plans for the show. Bawden wrote:

> Yes, our show must be a success – I told the Boy I thought we ought to exhibit between 75 and 100 things each. He jumped – He began 'But Bawden' – I said 'I think they ought to be mostly watercolours, don't you'? His jaw dropped and then he said 'No, I don't' – We sat in my bedroom and discussed the matter and the night deepened. He said 'I should like to spend a whole night walking towards the moon – good night'.

The exhibition took place in October 1927, and they each showed about twenty watercolours. Not one of the three artists went to the private view; they were too unsophisticated to know it was the expected thing to do. There were a few notices and a few sales; it was not what they had hoped for. But they were not discouraged for long, and for Ravilious certainly, and Bawden perhaps, landscape painting in time became the form of art about which they cared most deeply.

Chapter 4

When college days were ended, Ravilious had been offered a part-time teaching job at his old school of art in Eastbourne. This would provide a small but steady income, and as he would be able to stay with his parents in Eastbourne when necessary he could still keep his London studio for his freelance work. So he accepted.

One of his students, Diana Saintsbury-Green, has described his first day there:

> Eric Ravilious came to Eastbourne Art School in September 1925 – I was just beginning my second year. The teaching at the school was at a pretty low ebb. A few students did well in the life-class, but there was no stimulus from our teachers and nobody seemed to care whether we attended regularly or not. The illustration master steered us in the direction of 'art nouveau'. Our work was executed in pen and ink, with elaborate meaningless patterning of dots and squiggles. I don't remember seeing any but women students in the illustration class. It was this group of nice but rather uninspired young women that Eric Ravilious faced that morning at the beginning of term.
>
> I have a very clear picture of him as he entered the room, and stood looking at us rather apprehensively, hands in pockets and his square shoulders slightly hunched – the sight of us, clustered round the table was evidently too much for him, as without speaking, he suddenly turned and went out. I thought he was a new student, he looked so young, but M. who always knew everything, though she was a shy retiring student, told us that he had come to take Mr B.'s place – 'No more "art nouveau" I hope', she murmured.
>
> The first thing he did the following day was to break up the groups gathered round the tables. He brought us some drawings and wood-cuts, which he had purchased in Italy, simple line work which he preferred to the drawings of the Renaissance, and some monochrome reproductions of Sienese paintings, by Duccio and Sassetta for instance. We, who had been nurtured on Aubrey Beardsley by one master, and on Brangwyn by another, thought the reproductions strange and the wood-cuts uninteresting. He talked eagerly about them and we tried to respond.
>
> It soon became clear that he thought little of our efforts at illustration: that 'drawing out of our heads' was indeed *out*. We began to keep sketchbooks and were made to collect photographs to bolster our lack of knowledge. One morning he took some of us to the public library, and I came away with a book of Sienese painting which opened new doors for me. He encouraged us to read widely, and on discovering my ignorance of contemporary writers other than popular novelists, he lent me one or two Aldous Huxleys and a David Garnett. My love of

Hudson and Richard Jefferies I owe to him, and we were soon all reading *The Natural History of Selborne* . . . He had the eager curiosity of a young boy, and a most refreshing cool judgement. He was never our art *master* but rather the most stimulating and hard-working member of a group. He was a cheerful though absorbed person, and rather reserved in spite of appearing friendly. I don't know if we realized our good fortune then. He was so unassuming, and never tried to dominate or to show off.

Ravilious taught at Eastbourne for several years. A few of his students wanted to experiment with wood engraving. When *Desert* came out he showed them a copy and told them how depressed he was by the inking up of the fine lines on the block. Diana Saintsbury-Green continued:

Probably owing to this he began to 'open up' the patterned tooling which we practised on scraps of boxwood which he brought us – he would often engrave parts for us to copy. I think this was good teaching, for even in those days, wood was expensive. He merely showed us the best way to use our tools, but I never saw him draw for a student, though this was common practice in the life-class. His engraving students developed rapidly under tuition which was unique at that time.

In the summer he would take his students out into the country on sketching expeditions. Bicycling, or by Southdown bus, they went to such downland villages as Willingdon, Jevington, Wilmington or Alfriston. One of these students remembers Ravilious saying that his greatest ambition was to revive the English tradition of watercolour painting. Another has described his amusement at coming on a derelict *three*-seater earth-closet by the church at West Dean, and his making a drawing of it.

A certain anecdote perhaps best conveys the period flavour of a provincial art school of the mid-1920s. In the local paper there had been a letter complaining about 'shocking' scenes in the art school. An inspector rebuked the principal, and the staff were summoned to hear what had happened and this, Ravilious passed on to his own group: a window-cleaner, climbing up his ladder, had looked down into one of the studios and later reported, 'There, before my eyes, was a naked woman!'

Ravilious, although only a part-time member of staff, seems to have joined in some of the student's activities; for instance, for their production of an Elizabethan play, *The Careful Wife*, he designed the dresses for each girl playing a part, and was very firm that they were not to exchange them, this even when a red-haired girl thought she would look better in a black-and-white patterned dress, rather than the bright yellow and white one that Ravilious had decided she should wear.

But a new element was to come into his life before this. When he was at college, his friends had watched with detachment his constant falling in and out of love; he was easily moved by feminine beauty, but though a few of his love affairs had seemed serious enough, he had never yet got to the point of declaring his love.

Now, in his second year of teaching at Eastbourne, he fell in love with a student newly enrolled at the art school. Her name was Tirzah Garwood; she was eighteen and extraordinarily pretty. A painter friend of Eric's described her once as 'a stunner, with the long neck and slender grace of a Modigliani, and the aura and complexion of wild-rose petals'.

Tirzah Garwood in the 1920s.

She had dark hair and eyes, but a whiter skin than Modigliani's warm-complexioned girls.

She was the daughter of a retired lieutenant-colonel of the Royal Engineers, who had settled in Eastbourne with his wife and family of one son and four daughters. His son came second in the family and Tirzah third; hence her name, or nickname, as she had been christened Eileen, but was never called by it.

Colonel Garwood was in the habit of keeping a diary which recorded his own and his family's doings. Both parents had a strong sense of duty. Mrs Garwood, who was brought up as a Presbyterian and was strictly teetotal, seems to have been a very good needlewoman and to have made evening dresses for her daughters to wear to parties. She was in charge of the garden and the gardener and managed the flowers with great efficiency.

Colonel Garwood was kept busy with committee meetings of the British Legion and of the Board of Guardians; workhouses still existed in 1926, though they were soon to be abolished. He seems to have been a devoted father, with Tirzah perhaps his favourite daughter; his intellectual and artistic interests and prejudices were the conventional ones of his class and period; his real delight was in natural history – every bird's nest is noted in the diary.

In this respect Tirzah was like him. Although she was pretty, and had many admirers, she was not in the least vain or coquettish, and was always more interested in observing beetles or butterflies than in her own appearance. She was rather delicate and seems to have had to take to her bed fairly often. But there seems to have been plenty of gaiety in her life, dancing at the seaside hotels or on the pier with young men who were probably brother officers of John Garwood.

Looking through the colonel's diary we see that for 30 September 1926 the entry is 'Tirzah suddenly very keen and energetic about School of Art'; on 24 November 'Tirzah's first wood-block'.

Tirzah was not only very pretty, she was Ravilious's most promising student, and she took to wood engraving with great enthusiasm. By the autumn of 1927 she was exhibiting four engravings in the society of Wood-Engravers' London show. It was at about this time that we read in the diary, 'Tirzah spent the day with Reveillious [sic] (the young art-master), whom she brought to lunch and played tennis with afterwards.' This must have been Eric's first meeting with the Garwood family. There was later a very uncomfortable tea-party, when Ravilious met Tirzah's mother and all four daughters together; one of the sisters once described his sitting bolt upright on the very edge of his chair, and obviously very nervous. The family were all very loath to think of him as a possible suitor for Tirzah; it took a long time for him to win her, and indeed at one stage she turned him down.

The Ravilious family moved in different and humbler Eastbourne circles than the Garwoods, and in the 1920s class distinctions were rigid. By now, of course, Eric had largely left his family background behind, and so did not conform to either family's standards. He deeply resented Mrs Garwood's criticisms and contempt of the slightly different social customs he was used to, and at a time when he was urging his students to read Aldous Huxley, Colonel Garwood was writing in his diary – 'I read a foul modern book called *Attic Hay* by Huxley [*Antic Hay* was published in 1923]. It is in the most appalling bad taste.' So there was a difficult adjustment to be made on both sides, and even Eric's mother told him she thought it was a mistake to think of marrying into 'such a high-up family'.

Of course, the English middle classes have always looked upon art and artists with suspicion, and the Garwoods assumed that Eric's income would be meagre and uncertain and his life with Tirzah poverty-stricken.

But their greatest objection to him as a son-in-law was that they had already chosen an entirely suitable one, whom they expected Tirzah to marry when he came back to England on his next leave. He was the son of old family friends also living in Eastbourne, and there was 'an understanding' between him and Tirzah that they would in time be married. He was a clever young man, who had done well at Oxford and then gone into the Colonial Service. When Tirzah wrote and told him of his rival, he applied for, and was granted, special leave to come home to England to marry and bring her back to India.

It was a difficult decision for Tirzah, for though she had at first laughed at Eric, she had now begun to fall in love with him. She was also feeling more and more that her own art was important to her; she was already one of the star students of the art school, winning prizes for drawing as well as for engraving. She felt the narrowness of Eastbourne circles and decided to go and work in London as soon as it could be managed.

She went to stay at the Ladies' National Club in Hornton Street, in Kensington, which was a street away from two of her aunts; they were devoted to their nieces and had given a dance for them in London and had taken Tirzah winter-sporting. Not only these real aunts, but also an adopted one, the fiancée of an uncle of Tirzah's who had been killed in the First World War, had a house in the neighbourhood, and she invited Tirzah to meet her nephew James (usually called Jim) Richards. He had trained as an architect, but was just starting work as a writer on *The Architectural Review*. He already knew and admired Eric's work, so was delighted when Tirzah suggested bringing him to their next meeting, and they all became friends and saw a good deal of each other in the next years.

Well before all this, in 1928, Eric had started work on his first big commission for a mural decoration at Morley College in Lambeth.

The Refreshment Room at the Tate Gallery had lately been decorated with murals by a young artist called Rex Whistler, the whole scheme being paid for by the famous art dealer Sir Joseph Duveen. It had considerable success, was enjoyed by many visitors, and brought renown to Whistler, and to the Slade School where he had been trained. Professor Rothenstein, remembering that the task he had been set was 'to raise the prestige of the Royal College of Art', persuaded Duveen, who was a personal friend, to pay for another such venture, to be undertaken this time by some of the college students. Charles Aitken, director of the Tate at that time, recommended as a building requiring decoration the Georgian house in Lambeth into which Morley College for Working Men and Women had moved. In 1924 'it possessed a large Hall and a rather gloomy Refreshment Room, both needing the enhancement and stimulus of colour decoration. The activities of Morley College, with its throngs of workers seeking both knowledge and intellectual refreshment in their spare time, were exactly of the nature to arouse the sympathy of the promoters and of young artists.'

Six young artists, lately students at the Royal College, were asked to submit drawings to a committee, and three were chosen to carry out their

'A Lodging House' –
design for murals for the
Refreshment Room at
Morley College, 1929.
Pencil and watercolour.
16½" × 19½".
Anthony d'Offay

projects. A painting student called Cyril Mahoney was to do the decoration for the wall at the back of the stage in the large hall. The Refreshment Room on the basement floor was to have all its walls adorned by the two design students, Edward Bawden and Eric Ravilious, each taking on half of the wall space.

Rothenstein had asked them to do sketch designs for the restaurant, with London as the subject. Bawden chose London Bridge and Ravilious Trafalgar Square. Bawden has written: 'We decided to collaborate but even so, such a vast intractable subject was too much for inexperienced young men to grapple with'. Rothenstein rejected the sketches and suggested something on the lines of a fantasy, and that suggestion turned out to be an inspiration.

They made new drawings and sent them in to Rothenstein who wrote on 5 July to Ravilious, at the Eastbourne School of Art:

> I am perfectly delighted with the additional drawings you sent me – I have written to Sir Joseph Duveen and asked him to come and see what has been sent in – Mr Aitken is coming next Monday – I have little doubt that your and Bawden's designs for the Refreshment Room will be accepted. They will certainly have the entire backing of Mr Wellington and myself.

On 10 July he was able to write:

> You will be glad to know that your and Bawden's designs have been accepted and were warmly appreciated by the representatives of Morley College, Mr Aitken of the Tate and Mr Pearson the Architect. . . . The important thing, since you want to start work in September, is to settle the preparation for the walls – I do not know whether you contemplate painting straight on to the plaster or having the walls lined with canvas, in which case, of course, you could work away from the College.

*The two artists at work –
this photograph of Eric
Ravilious and Edward
Bawden working on the
Morley College murals
was published in the
Evening Standard
Monday 3 February 1930.*

They chose to work directly on to the plaster walls and, at Professor Tristram's suggestion, to paint with oil colours mixed with wax, and then thinned with turpentine.

They were to be paid by the day, that is, paid for every day or half day that they worked on the murals; there was no deadline for finishing them and they could take time off when they needed to. It was a big job and took them almost two years to finish. They were helped and encouraged by the sympathy of Mrs Hubback, the principal of Morley College.

Here is the official description of the mural paintings:

In the Refreshment Room on the basement floor Mr Bawden and Mr Ravilious have worked in concert, but each is responsible for his own portions of wall space. They have aimed at providing plenty of things interesting to look at and intriguing to unravel for people sitting scattered about the room. The nucleus idea – scenes from Shakespeare's Plays and old English Dramas, Miracle Plays, and Pantomime – was provided by the historic association of Morley College with the Old Vic Theatre. The different episodes or scenes are given considerable sharpness of detail and colour, and as wall paintings may be said to bear a relation to present day illustration rather similar to that of English mediaeval wall painting to contemporary manuscripts. Certain fixed conditions – architectural features such as doors, hatch-openings and mouldings – have been considered in setting out proportions and horizontals, and these, together with a considered colour scheme, are relied upon to give sufficient unity to the different walls. Recurring views of the interiors of theatres and other buildings are devices for isolating the scenes, and for creating a continuous design with an architectural frame-work and structure. The scheme is carried out in a spirit of free fantasy, no attempt is made to burden the design with a

logical or chronological sequence.

The designers have chosen the plays for no other reason than they liked them, and have allowed themselves to improvise freely, to mix observations with intention and fun, and evoke an atmosphere no closer to every day reality than the life of the stage or the life of dreams.

The happy thing about the paintings is the airy freedom of the figures dancing or acting or floating or flying in and out of the different open-sided structures – these last surely inspired by memories of Italian frescoes by such artists as Bernardo Daddi and Masolino. Ravilious managed to bring in his Wilmington Giant on the hills seen behind the tall arcading of a scene from Ben Jonson's Masque of *Cynthia's Revels*. It is also characteristic that for one scene he forgot all about Elizabethan drama and painted something that fits perfectly into the general scheme, but depicts a fantasy about his own life and feelings of that moment. The front wall has been removed from a six-roomed modern boarding – or doll's – house, each room belonging to a different inhabitant. In the top attics, a girl lies dreaming in bed, a poet is visited by the muse. On the next floor a father and a father-in-law talk about the young couple in the opposite room, who are welcoming the vicar. The girl is a charming portrait of Tirzah; in fact, all the girls are Tirzah – her back view is climbing the stairs, and she is practising the piano in the basement. In the kitchen a friend of theirs, Bowk (Beryl Bowker, who had been a student in the Painting School at the Royal College), is moving an aspidistra. There is a greenhouse, attached to the wall, and gods and goddesses float about in the sky.

On 30 January 1930, shortly before the opening, Rothenstein wrote in a letter to Ravilious: 'I cannot express my happiness in your wall, each time I see it, so full of beauty, wit and poetry as it is – I hope many will feel as I do about these admirable paintings.'

'Bowk' in the kitchen of 'A Lodging House', part of the Morley College murals.

'Tennis' door panels painted in oils by Ravilious for the Music Room in Sir Geoffrey Fry's Portman Court flat, 1930. There is a photograph of the panels **in situ** reproduced in **Studio** September 1933. City of Bristol Museum & Art Gallery

The date for the opening was fixed for 6 February 1930, and was to be performed by the Prime Minister, Mr Stanley Baldwin. His private secretary, Sir Geoffrey Fry, came beforehand to settle all the arrangements with Ravilious and Bawden, and he of course met them again at the opening ceremony to which a great many people came. In his speech Mr Baldwin started by alluding to the fact that he was a nephew by marriage of the painter Burne-Jones, thus guaranteeing his suitability for the job of declaring the wall paintings open to the public, and then went on to talk politics.

Sir Geoffrey Fry was a distinguished civil servant and a patron of art and artists, and he and his wife delighted to entertain promising young men of talent at their Wiltshire country house and in London. He was impressed by Ravilious at once and very admiring of his work, and was soon commissioning 'Tennis' door panels for his London flat in Portman Square. His friendship was to become important in Eric and Tirzah's life, and until they left London, they saw a lot of each other.

In his diary for 1930 Colonel Garwood wrote on 9 January: 'A letter from T saying that she had made her definite choice between her two suitors'; and on 13 January: 'Two not unexpected letters explaining the situation from Ravillious [sic] and Tirzah'. On 14 January: 'I wrote an answer to Ravilious in the evening.' This is the first time the name Ravilious is spelt correctly; there had been a variety of versions, Reveillous, Revilliez, Ravilliers, since that first entry in the diary in 1926. Tirzah decided that the wedding should be in July, and the date was fixed for 5 July and was to be in London, as announced in *The Times* on 23 May. Tirzah gave up her room in Hornton Street, and Mrs Garwood became very busy with the trousseau. Wedding presents began to arrive. Geoffrey Fry sent Eric the complete works of Max Beerbohm, and Rothenstein gave an Indian painting. He was the only wedding guest to come in morning-coat and top hat but was not at all embarrassed. The wedding service in a Presbyterian church was short; Edward Bawden acted as best man. The crowded reception was held at Tirzah's aunts' house in Argyll Road. The young couple, accompanied by Tirzah's dog, Charles, went off to a honeymoon in Cornwall.

Eric and Tirzah. Two portraits in oils by Phyllis Dodd, 1929. Eric – 13¾" × 11½"; Tirzah – 23½" × 19½".
Ravilious Family

Chapter 5

Eric and Tirzah Ravilious started their married life in a top floor flat at 5 Stratford Road, Kensington. Eric had been offered a one-day-a-week job teaching in the Design School at the Royal College, so he took this on instead of the Eastbourne teaching. He also went a few times a term to teach wood engraving at the Ruskin School of Art in Oxford, where he succeeded John Nash. One of his students reported that Nash and Ravilious held their engraving tools in different ways. Ravilious worked with his forefinger held along the length of the tool, which is not the orthodox way of a professional engraver, but perhaps it helped him to develop his very free and direct way of cutting.

Teaching was a side-line, of course, as his main occupation was his own work. That August of 1930, in a letter to Cecilia Dunbar Kilburn about the bookplate for the Indian Rajah, Eric wrote: 'We had done so little work for such a long time (what with holidays in Cornwall, weekends away, and what not) we are now both as busy as we have ever been in either of our lives.'

If he had not already started work on a new *Twelfth Night* for the Golden Cockerel Press, he was to do so very soon. It was his third book for this Press, and much the most important. It was a formidable undertaking.

It is a large but fairly slim book. On opening it one sees, first of all, a full-page illustration. Underneath the title of the play, which is printed in black capitals, is an engraving of Maria meeting the Clown in a formal garden, flanked by two arbours, and printed in brown. All this is enclosed in a leafy border, one side the reverse of the other, and printed in a dark grey colour. The whole design is beautifully balanced, light and airy and strong.

A decision was made to print the text throughout in black ink, but with each illustration in one or other of two colours – a purple-brown or a blue-grey; this was not Ravilious's choice and he was disappointed when he saw the result. The brown colour holds its own against the black of the text, because as a reddish colour it appears to come forward, but the blue-grey seems to retire into the page, and the illustrations in this colour seem weakened in relation to the text. It was an enterprising idea to try the two colours, but a mistake to choose them finally.

Except for the title page and the decorated list of *dramatis personae*, all the illustrations are half page, with many head-and tail-pieces, and decorations in the margins. The artist has been concerned to keep the cutting much more open than in his earlier books for the Golden Cockerel Press, and to make use in places of a fine dark outline, like that in a wood cut, particularly for the faces and hands. The figures are kept to the same scale throughout, which gives a pleasant sense of unity to the pages as one turns them over. In the illustrations the figures are related to a back-

Withdrawn from

Cleveland Inst. of Art Library

ground, but in some of the marginal decorations, an isolated figure – Viola, perhaps, about to enter – hovers as it were in the wings.

Ravilious was not particularly interested in the way human emotions and relationships are expressed by people's attitudes and movements, nor did he revel in oddities and awkwardnesses of appearance. Sir Andrew's absurdity and Sir Toby's uproariousness are subordinated to a feeling for the whole scene, in which the setting is quite as important dramatically as the actors. And both are above all related to their place on the page.

The considerable research he had already done on the Elizabethan period was of course invaluable, and it must have been a great help to know where best to look for reference for costumes and for particular architectural backgrounds. There is a splendid inventiveness in the different kinds of arcading, doorways and courtyards, garden arbours, and yew and box hedges cut into fanciful shapes; and the range of floor patternings is specially telling.

All this represents an immense amount of work. There were in the end twelve illustrations and twelve or more head- and tail-pieces and decorations for the margins, as well as the large title-page, and list of *dramatis personae*. Besides the engraving of each of these, there was also the clearing away of the box-wood left round the edges of the designs, and particularly the intricate borders, which would print unless removed. As Eric's best student of engraving, Tirzah was able to help with this.

Once a cut is made in the surface of a box-wood block, it cannot be erased, but it is possible for a part of a block to be removed, and for a new piece of wood of exactly the same size to be cunningly glued in its place by a highly skilled block maker. This must have happened to the title-page illustration, as there still exists a proof of a first version, with a different arbour to the left of Maria.

The blockmaker was Mr Stanley Lawrence of Red Lion Court, and without his firm T. N. Lawrence, the only one to survive from the heyday of commercial wood engraving in the Victorian era, the revival of wood engraving could never have taken place. All the members of the Society of Wood Engravers found their way up the narrow stairs to Lawrence's old-fashioned office, to buy beautiful box-wood blocks cut to the size they asked for, as well as the inks, rollers, tools and Japanese papers that they needed.

In their prospectus for 1931, the Golden Cockerel Press announced their books for the year. At the head of the list comes 'Twelfth Night, or What you Will, by William Shakespeare', described as 'decorated by Eric Ravilious, and the largest volume yet attempted by the Press. The format is to be Crown Folio, and an example of the engraving, a reduced reproduction of the title page is shown. The paper will be Kelmscott handmade, the type 14 pt Golden Cockerel face, and each volume hand-bound by Messrs Sangorski and Sutcliffe in quarter niger, buckram sides. The edition will be limited to 500 copies, which include all printed, whether for sale or presentation in England or the United States of America. Price 5 guineas.' This prospectus had Ravilious engravings on its cover, both front and back, showing the Golden Cockerel crowing or carrying Robert Gibbings up towards heaven.

The autumn 1931 lists of the Golden Cockerel Press had as its first paragraph: 'The Gold Standard has gone, but not the Golden Cockerel Standards'. Some new books are announced for the next year, and a change in the plan for *Twelfth Night*, as follows:

The two versions of
'Maria meeting the
Clown' from **Twelfth**
Night *(The Golden*
Cockerel Press, 1930).
The top version is the one
which appears in the
book.

It has been decided to alter, in a small degree, the format of 'Twelfth Night', now in course of preparation: instead of the size being Crown Folio, it will be uniform in measurement with 'The Four Gospels', that is 13¼ × 9¼ ins. The paper has been specially made for the Press by Joseph Batchelor & Sons, and bears a unique watermark. There will not be so many full-page decorations, but there will be a larger number of smaller engravings. The edition will be limited to 325 copies, and the price will be Three Guineas.

Changing most of the planned whole-page illustrations to half-page probably suited the engraver better, and therefore the look of the book, but the announcement was rather ominous for the Press.

At the start of the project in 1930 Eric had written to Robert Gibbings: 'I much look forward to this magnum opus of mine', and a few months later Gibbings was writing, 'I hope very much the volume is going to set a new standard for us as well as for everybody else'. But by June a year later, soon after its publication, Eric was writing in answer to a letter from his publisher, 'I am very sorry the play does not seem to be selling as well as it might: there is something called a 'depression' at work just now'. In February 1932 Robert Gibbings went to the West Indies, and came home to find the slump had really hit England. The morning's post brought nothing but cancellations instead of orders. He carried on as long as he dared, and then, as he wrote at the time, 'sold the Golden Cockerel Press to those who were in a position to make of it a part-time concern and keep it alive until prosperity returns'.

The new owners, Christopher Sandford and his partner, Owen Rutter, were to ask Ravilious to do more work for the Golden Cockerel later on, but Ravilious's next engraving job was for a Birmingham firm of printers called the Kynoch Press. Its director was Herbert Simon, brother of Oliver Simon of the Curwen Press.

Every year they printed a *Kynoch Press Note Book*, with decorations by a different artist. The one for 1932 was ornamented with charming little stock electrotyped wood cuts from the type founders. Ravilious was asked to make engravings for the 1933 *Note Book*. He planned that every other page of the diary should have a little engraving as a heading, the subject related to the season of the year: a kettle boiling on the hob in January, pancakes being tossed in a pan in February, a bare-branched tree beside a village church for March, April showers and so on, culminating in December's scene of snowflakes falling, now white spots against dark trees and floods, or grey ones against white sky and fallen snow. These all have a very personal and delightful quality, and have often been reproduced in other contexts since.

In spite of the deepening slump, the success of the Morley College Murals had brought in an important commission. In 1933 a new Midland Railway hotel was being built at Morecambe, with the hope of attracting tourists to explore the area, particularly the Lake District. The architect was Oliver Hill, and for some reason the hotel was being put up in a great hurry, with the opening date already fixed for 12 July. Ravilious had been asked to design and execute a mural for the circular tearoom and bar; Eric Gill had been asked to do one in the main dining-room, and his son-on-law Denis Tegetmeier was making a pictorial map of the environment for another room.

The Raviliouses arrived first on 10 April and found lodgings at Hey-

Decorations from the 1933 Kynoch Press Note Book.

sham. They started work in the hotel at once, although workmen were still busy finishing the building. Tirzah's diary – a Kynoch Press one – for 14 April says, 'found walls would have to be stripped as paint isn't safe – 2 days' work to come off'; the following days have notes like 'Roof flooded at Hotel, walls and ceiling dripping wet', 'wall still peeling', 'first coat of paint on patches'. Then, in Eric's writing, 'this part of wall mended for *third* time.' On 11 May Tirzah wrote, 'Eric Gill and his assistant arrived last night and have drawn out their design'; for 22 May, 'ceiling wet again owing to ventilator leak'; 30 May, 'floormen hammered so had to give up'.

On 3 June the architect turned up and seemed to think it was the artists' fault that the wall's surface was so unsatisfactory. This continued; on 5

Above and below *'Day' and 'Night' – the circular tearoom and bar as decorated by Eric and Tirzah at the Midland Railway Hotel, Morecambe, 1933.* **The Architectural Review**

November 5th 1933.
Pencil and watercolour.
28½" × 38½". Signed
and dated. This was the
most expensive painting
in the 1933 Zwemmer
exhibition – 25 guineas.
Private Collection

June the diary notes 'patched one crack down left wall – Another bad crack appeared right wall' – and so on, a recurring theme.

Every other week Eric had to go back to London for his two days of teaching at the Royal College. It must have been a nightmarish time for them both, as Tirzah shared in the actual painting of the wall. There is one cheerful note in her diary: 'A man in a bus gave me a passion-flower.'

Eric got very worried about the unsatisfactory surface he had to work on, and consulted Eric Gill, whom he already knew through the Golden Cockerel Press. It seemed clear that there had not been enough time for the wall to dry out, but the date for completion had to be kept, and the formal opening of the hotel was carried out by Lord Derby, with a speech from Sir Josiah Stamp and various other grandees.

The wall continued to crack in places and to need patching; in December Eric Gill was writing to Ravilious:

I was up at Morecambe last Sunday to see Denis T. I heard you had been there – I am terribly sorry about the Tea Room – I wish I knew what to suggest. The proper thing of course would be for the Railway Company to pay you handsomely to renovate it (a job which it ought to be possible to get done by an expert assistant) but I suppose there is not the least chance of that. It seems a frightful shame to even talk of whitewashing it out, but can you possibly leave it as it is?

In the following March Eric and Tirzah had one more go at the wall. They stayed in the hotel this time, although it was not yet properly open and there was only a skeleton staff. Here their friend J. M. Richards joined them, as he was convalescing in the sea air after an operation.

One evening, in search of entertainment, they went to the little seaside theatre where there was to be a display of boxing. They took their seats, and when the curtain rose were delighted to see painted on the backcloth another audience facing them. Row upon row they sat, with the mayor and corporation in all their regalia, seated in the front row. The boxers fought in front of this, a surrealist touch that Eric and Tirzah and Jim all enjoyed.

The wall was now dry enough to be patched up satisfactorily. J. M. Richards has described it as 'one of Eric's gaily ingenious designs, composed of stylized recreational scenes, with a background of sea and sky, fluttering flags and fireworks'.

All his life, fireworks were an important and special source of inspiration for Eric's work, and were made use of in many different ways. By now he and Tirzah had moved from Kensington to Hammersmith, but not before Eric had painted an elaborate watercolour of *Bonfire Night*, as watched from the roof of their house in Stratford Road. He had found also that the white line of the engraving tools could be used most effectively for expressing the moving linear curves and starry patterns of fireworks, giving life and sparkle to many of the intricate engraved designs and decorations that he made for publishers; these are quite distinctive and unlike the work of any other artist – a kind of abstract art.

The move to Hammersmith gave Eric a new choice of subjects to paint; the flat was at the end of Weltje Road, and the bay window of their living-room looked out across Upper Mall to the Thames. The *Stork* training ship was moored opposite their window, and Eric painted several watercolours of it. The river was still clean enough to bathe in, and friends of the Raviliouses, the painters Gin and Raymond Coxon, used to have bathing parties from their garden in Hammersmith Terrace, just round the corner. Another neighbour in Hammersmith was the architect Maxwell Fry. He has described a mural Eric did for him at this time as 'an etched design on black glass, a lovely delicate, intricate sort of rose-window', shown at an Art and Industries Exhibition at the Royal Academy. Edward Bawden was also living in the neighbourhood now, but the Blisses had moved out to Blackheath, and Bowk had married a *Daily Herald* journalist called Robert Sinclair and lived in Upper Gloucester Place, where she painted pleasant pictures of Regent's Park, gave lively parties, and was a fountainhead of art-world gossip: Charlotte Epton was

The Stork, Hammersmith
Watercolour. 15" × 22½". Signed. This was first exhibited at Zwemmer's in 1933. Towner Art Gallery, Eastbourne

teaching art at Cheltenham Ladies' College and was engaged to Edward Bawden. The only one of the old circle still intermittently living in a Radcliffe Road studio was Cecilia Dunbar Kilburn.

Every spring, of course, there was the Hammersmith festival of the Oxford and Cambridge Boat Race, for which everyone with a view of the river from their house gave a Boat Race Party. The moment of drama when the thin, pointed prows of the boats first appear out from under Hammersmith Bridge, with the spreading swarm of little steamers and motor-boats following behind, was one that Eric specially enjoyed.

Some account of other leisure activities can be found in Tirzah's engagement book for 1933. The Raviliouses went to the private views of both their friends and their seniors. Those of Michael Rothenstein, the Seven and Five Group, Henry Moore, Sickert, Enid Marx, the New English Art Club, Gilbert Spencer and Vanessa Bell are mentioned. They visited the Blisses at Blackheath and the Percy Hortons at Dulwich. There were engagements with the Christopher Sandfords, with John G. Murray – 'marvellous dinner' – and Tom Balston, all publishers who commissioned work from Ravilious. They had been invited to the Queen's Hall to watch the filming of a scene from *The Constant Nymph* and found themselves being filmed as students at the back of the orchestra.

The initials G.F. appear quite often in the engagement book. Geoffrey Fry had now moved from his Portman Square flat to Sloane House, in Chelsea. Tirzah and Eric went there often. Lady Fry, whose name was Alethea, seems to have been rather delicate. She was laid up with a twisted ankle when the Raviliouses were invited for the weekend to the Frys' beautiful Georgian country house at Oare, in Wiltshire.

This first visit was rather alarming, and they found it a slightly bewildering experience, especially at meals. Eric once described the sort of thing that might happen: 'The butler will solemnly bring in a fresh knife and fork to replace those used out-of-course. At Oare once I managed to spill a glass of Burgundy so wildly that they had to bring in a sponge to wipe up the mess. I didn't mind a lot and Geoffrey went on talking all the time as if nothing had happened; a quite perfect host would have said *something* – in a perfectly level voice and left it at that.' Nevertheless they did enjoy the visit. At a later time Eric once spoke of Fry as 'the only man I know not as yet roped in to the general zoo (of the Art World) so relations with him are particularly free and easy.'

By the summer of 1930 Bawden and Ravilious had both been feeling a longing to do more landscape painting and to have, if they could find it, a permanent base in the country. So one day they took a train to Great Dunmow, in Essex, hired bicycles, and set off to look for an empty cottage that they could rent and share for holidays and weekends. They had no luck in the first villages they passed through, but as they cycled up the little rise to the centre of Great Bardfield, at the top of the hill, next to the police station, they saw a small square Georgian house, built of black and red bricks, and with a white door in the middle. The panes of the windows to the left of this door had been dabbed with circles of whitewash – a promising sign? They had cups of tea in a little sweet-shop and asked about the house they had just passed. They were told it was called Brick House, and that a retired stewardess from a liner lived alone there. It seemed it might be worth asking her to let them part of her house. Full of hope, the two artists knocked on the door, which was opened by the stewardess. After some talk she agreed to let them half the house for a low rent. They could have two rooms on the ground floor, and two above with a share of the kitchen and the primitive amenities.

This was to be the beginning of a very fruitful time for both artists. They moved into their country quarters as soon as they could. They all enjoyed the country sights and sounds and the feelings of belonging there. There was time to look at butterflies – both Charlotte Bawden and Tirzah had keen eyes for spotting the rarer kinds; to watch the swallows building their nests in the portico above their own front door; to see, after a deluge of rain, the road outside covered with hundreds of little frogs; and to notice at night how much larger the moon looked than in London. All this was the most delightful enlargement of experience, which they expressed in their work. Nearly all the engravings Ravilious did for the *Kynoch Press Note Book* have Bardfield subjects, and Bawden's *Gardener's Diary* for 1937, which he decorated for Country Life, celebrates the fascinating plants which by this date were growing in the Brick House garden that Edward had planned and cultivated so beautifully.

Landscape painting was their chief object. Tirzah once wrote this about her husband and Edward Bawden:

> The garden and country round Bardfield inspired them both and they competed with one another in conditions of various hardships, such as ghastly weather, or working with the sun bang in their eyes. They painted several pictures very early in the morning from the roof of their house, and on one occasion had to come down, nearly overpowered by the smell of kippers cooking for breakfast. Bawden thought you ought to finish the painting on the spot, but Eric might do half his at home. They always worked very hard and got up very early in the morning.

Brick House was not in a good state of repair when they first lived there, but they gradually renovated and decorated it. By the time the Bawdens left London and went to Great Bardfield permanently, they had acquired the whole house, and they made it beautiful. But earlier than

'*Brick House Garden Party*' – Eric and the poet Tom Hennell are on the left, Edward Bawden and Tirzah Ravilious on the right. Edward Bawden produced this illustration for Ambrose Heath's **Good Food** (Faber & Faber, 1932). Towner Art Gallery, Eastbourne

Garden Path
9 January 1934.
Watercolour. 16¾″ ×
23¼″ Signed. Exhibited
at Zwemmer's in 1936,
this painting shows the
back garden at Brick
House.
Towner Art Gallery,
Eastbourne

this, in the March before her wedding in 1932, Charlotte was writing to her great friend Gwyneth Lloyd-Thomas, a don at Girton:

> Edward and Rav are at Bardfield this week decorating the 'Victorian' room. They are threatening to paint stags' horns and trophies of the chase in suitable positions on the wall, and forget-me-nots and pansies round the fireplace, but I think Rav will keep a discreet hand over Edward's rococo spirit.

A technique that Bawden was exploring brilliantly was linocutting. He had made some very original wallpapers in this way, and the Curwen Press had used his designs to produce printed pattern papers. Wallpapers would be useful for Brick House, and Charlotte and Tirzah decided to make experiments on their own with 'marbled' papers once much used by book-binders. Edward had done a course on book-binding at the Sir John Cass Institute and could describe the marbling he had done there.

They made some very attractive papers, with freer kinds of pattern than usual, but these could not be continuous as on rolls of wallpaper. They made very good patchwork for walls, and they also had lampshades and waste-paper baskets made professionally and covered with their papers; these were accepted for sale by the Little Gallery, which was an enterprising shop started by Miss Muriel Rose in 1928 to show the work of her chosen craftsmen and craftswomen in sympathetic surroundings. She had collected a clientèle of customers who shared her fiercely high standards of tests and workmanship.

Another new gallery, which had exhibitions chiefly of paintings, was the Zwemmer Gallery in Litchfield Street, just round the corner from the Zwemmer bookshop, whose owner had opened the small gallery in emulation of a gallery and bookshop in New York run with great success by a Mr Weyer. The young man appointed to be in charge of the Zwemmer Gallery was Robert Wellington, the son of Hubert Wellington, the registrar at the Royal College. As the gallery went in for new young artists,

The device from the Private View invitation to Eric's exhibition at the Zwemmer Gallery, which ran from 24 November – 16 December 1933. Engraved on wood.

this link with the college was of benefit to all of them.

There was an interesting mixed show held in April 1932 called 'Room and Book', which was opened to coincide with the publication of Paul Nash's book of the same name. Both exhibition and book were concerned to reveal the new ideas of new artists as expressed in paintings or pottery, sculpture or weaving, wallpapers, furniture, rugs or printed textiles, all suitable in scale for the setting of a private house. Edward Bawden exhibited wallpapers and small pattern papers; Eric showed a design for a Cactus House, which the critic of the *London Mercury* described as 'outstanding in subtle humour and dexterity of treatment'.

But it was their first one-man shows of paintings planned by the Zwemmer gallery for the autumn of 1933, that were to be of greater importance to them both; Bawden's private view was on 4 October and his show had a considerable success. The *Times* art critic, Charles Marriott, wrote that his pictures had the 'tang of water-cress' which brought two buyers into the gallery next morning. Altogether twenty-four paintings were sold.

Ravilious's show was called simply 'An Exhibition of Water-Colour Drawings', and the cards, printed in black and red and ornamented with an engraved device – one of his best – were sent out inviting people to the private view on 24 November 1933.

There were thirty-seven drawings in the show. The subjects were varied, but such titles as *Engine in Winter, Engine Yard, Tractors, Buoys and Grappling Hook* tell of his preoccupations at this time, and were mostly drawn near Bardfield, as were *Village School, Newt Pond* and *Pink Farm*, while *Marrow Bed* and *Marlborough Downs* were drawn at Oare.

By the end of the show twenty pictures had been sold. It was a promising beginning.

Farm Implements 1932. Watercolour. 15″ × 18½″. Signed and dated. This was probably the picture exhibited as **Engines in Winter** at the 1933 Zwemmer exhibition. Private Collection

Chapter 6

One of the visitors to Edward Bawden's first show at the Zwemmer Gallery who found it particularly exciting was Peggy Angus, who had been a fellow student in the Design School at the Royal College. She was working in the country, and was not able to get up to London to see the show until the last day; she longed to buy one of the paintings, but by then they were nearly all sold. She also knew that she could not possibly afford to pay for it, so she wrote to Bawden, telling him of her delight in his watercolours, and saying how much she would like to buy one if he would accept an arrangement for her to pay by instalments of £1 a month. Perhaps she might be allowed to come and choose a watercolour. Bawden wrote back and invited her for a weekend to Brick House.

Peggy chose a weekend at the beginning of January and arrived on the Friday. When she found herself inside Brick House, she was completely bowled over by the flowering of inventiveness in decorations on every wall, ceiling or floor. As she remembers it, there were lozenges of marbled papers, repeated as patchwork patterns in the hall and passage; the dining-room had a wallpaper of rubbings from brasses, the parlour made her feel she was in a cane structure, with bird-cages and birds everywhere, and a bedroom had become a striped tent, draped up to a centre point. The room she slept in had brass rubbings under painted Gothic Revival arcading, somewhat spidery in character; on its walls Edward Bawden had made a screen of beautifully arranged pages from illustrated letters, with tantalizing indiscretions here and there. It was not in the least like any house Peggy had ever been in before.

She also much enjoyed looking out of the windows and recognizing the subjects of some of Bawden's paintings that she had so much admired in his show. It was all very exhilarating, as was the company and the conversation. Peggy was very pleased to meet Eric again. She had only seen him once since college days, when they had run into each other on Waterloo Bridge, and Eric had said that he needed to make a drawing of a grand piano and was trying to find one. She was delighted to meet Tirzah for the first time; Charlotte, of course, had been a fellow student at the college. The other visitor to Brick House that weekend was an attractive young artist called Diana Low; she had been Charlotte's most promising pupil at Cheltenham College and had studied painting since then at the Slade and with William Nicholson.

It happened that Edward was much preoccupied with work that week-end, and Charlotte was a great preparer of delicious meals, so exploring the neighbourhood and showing its beauties to Peggy and Diana was undertaken by the Raviliouses.

The next afternoon was warm for mid-winter, and rather misty. The four of them made for the little plantation of cricket-bat willows nearby, through which the river Pant flowed. The fog thickened as they reached

*Talbot-Darracq 1935.
Watercolour. 18" × 22".
This painting, exhibited
in 1936, demonstrates
Ravilious's fascination
with old and abandoned
machinery.
R. C. Tuely*

its banks, and Peggy, who was given to such exhibitionist gestures, tore off her clothes and jumped into the cold waters of the Pant, crying, 'Come on, let's bathe, no one can see us in this mist.' Eric, who always responded to a challenge, at once did the same, and so did Diana: Tirzah, with more experience of illness than the others, was very disapproving, and imagined them catching bad colds, if not pneumonia, and giving trouble all round. She stayed on the bank, watching the bathers – pale apparitions in the yellow fog – splashing in the river and then running about on the bank playing catch as catch can. They came back to the house very pleased with their exploit, and no ill-effects followed.

Peggy had seen more of Bawden's watercolours and particularly liked one of Newhaven Cliffs, which she was allowed to buy on her instalment system. It had been a lovely weekend, and she warmly invited them all to come to her cottage in Sussex. The Bawdens said they would like to come sometime, but were too busy at the moment, but Eric was delighted at the idea and said that he and Tirzah would like to come soon.

Peggy's cottage was in the heart of the South Downs. Her first teaching job after leaving college – she had passed the teaching course examinations very successfully – was at Nuneaton. Her next was at Eastbourne, where instead of living in the town she found a lodging in a cowman's cottage near Alfriston. It was from there that she discovered the joys of exploring the South Downs; when she was next offered a teaching job in London, at the Henrietta Barnett School in Hampstead, she was delighted to accept it and to be going to live again in London, but she was also reluctant to leave the Sussex countryside. She decided to look for a deserted or even derelict cottage that she could use for holidays, and she found one near Lewes, called Furlongs.

Eric and Tirzah went to Furlongs for the first time in the spring of

This Beatonesque snap 'à la Sitwell' was taken by Ishbel Macdonald, 8 September 1933. **From the top, clockwise** *Jim Richards, Eric Ravilious, Helen Binyon, Bert Kelly.*

Opposite:

Waterwheel *1934. Watercolour. 18″ × 21½″. Signed. Exhibited at Ravilious's 1936 show. Private Collection*

Alpha Cement Works *1934. Watercolour. 19¾″ × 22½″. Exhibited 1936. City of Manchester Art Galleries*

1934. Peggy met them at Victoria and after changing at Lewes they took the train on to Glynde. Here they got out, laden with rucksacks and painting gear, and walked on through the village. They stopped at the farm to collect the milk, and then went on until they reached and crossed the main Lewes to Eastbourne road. They continued along a narrowing tree-lined lane, until they reached an open field, with the swelling slopes of the chalk Downs beyond, their rounded tops bare against the sky. They turned to the right, along a deeply rutted track, past a little copse, over which towered the wheel of a creaking wind pump; on its vane the mysterious word 'DANDO'. Ahead and still some way off, they saw the cottage; it stood squarely above the track, with a few old barns and a walnut tree half hidden behind. It was built of flints with brick corners and a narrow slate roof. Stark and plain, with no picturesque gables or thatched roof, it seemed to guard the way to the Down behind.

Eric was enchanted by it all and saw subjects for his paintings everywhere. The spaciousness and breadth of views of land and of skies excited him after the more domestic scenes he had been painting in Essex, and he felt he had come to his own country, though he had never before been to this particular stretch of the South Downs, with Mount Caburn to the north, and Firle Beacon to the east.

He also enjoyed the simple camping life at the cottage, the informality and the picnic arrangements; no carpets to object to muddy boots, for instance, and a less firm line between indoors and outdoors behaviour. This first visit was a great success and he was to come back many times.

Other visitors came and went; John Piper and Myfanwy Evans, Jim Richards, Robert Wellington, and Peggy's great friend at school, Ishbel MacDonald, the daughter of Ramsay MacDonald, the Labour politician and sometime Prime Minister (when Peggy was living at her cowman's cottage near Alfriston she had found 10 Downing Street a very useful place to go to for a bath). There were certainly others, but the ex-college student who came most regularly to paint was Percy Horton. He had won a Royal Exhibition in Painting and came to the Royal College the

same year as Bawden and Ravilious, but was a few years older. He had been a student at the Brighton Art School during the 1914 war and, like Eric, loved the Sussex landscape.

He and Eric were both musical and enjoyed songs and singing; with Peggy they had a fine repertory between them. The evenings at Furlongs would sometimes be spent in singing Elizabethan rounds taught by Percy – the favourites were 'Slaves to the world shall be tossed in a blanket', and 'Wind gentle evergreen to form a shade/Around the tomb where Sophocles is laid.' The small cottage sitting-room, with a fire of sticks and broken branches gathered from the woods, and lit by an oil lamp, was agreeably cosy after a day painting outdoors in April.

Furlongs was only about ten miles from Eastbourne, and from time to time some of the Garwood family would come and call. They deeply disapproved of Peggy, whom they called the Red Angus (she had travelled to the Soviet Union the previous summer with a group of enthusiastic Socialists), and they couldn't understand the attractions of such an un-picturesque and uncomfortable cottage. A car approaching Furlongs could be seen from a long way off, so it could be the signal for Eric and Peggy to make a hurried flight onto the Downs.

The only one of the different artists staying there who was not much interested in painting landscapes was Tirzah, though she sometimes made exquisite studies of objects she had brought indoors. The second time the Raviliouses came they brought with them more painting materials and Tirzah's marbling apparatus and sheets of Michallet paper. She set all this up and was soon making charming patterned papers; some of the plum-coloured ones she used to paper the wall in the Furlongs kitchen.

In other ways the appearance of the cottage was gradually altering. There would be expeditions to junk shops in Lewes led by Eric, who knew a lot about 'junking', learnt from his family's antique shop; they came back once with a large square-cornered Victorian mirror, which fitted exactly into the recess of the wall next to the kitchen range. He found and bought some black bentwood chairs, with round cane seats and longer legs than usual – the kind of chairs that used to be put out for the use of customers sitting at the counters of drapers shops; he also decided that a sort of dumb-waiter would be useful to draw on.

Eric liked to get up very early, occasionally at sunrise, and paint all the morning. After a picnic lunch he might have a short sleep and then paint again by the afternoon and evening light. He usually worked on a drawing-board which would take a Royal size sheet of paper, and Tirzah had made him a canvas satchel large enough to carry it. He had a light sketching easel at which he could work standing, or he might sit with the board on his knees.

Possibly the special qualities of his paintings came from the way he could keep his vision of whatever had first struck him and made him choose that subject. This would inevitably change as the day went on and the light altered, yet he did not often lose or dissipate the intensity of his first vision, and so communicated his excitement about it to the spectator. Later on he achieved this by working more from memory at home on a drawing begun at the place of discovery.

The first subject he chose to paint at Furlongs was the iron wind-pump rising up above the trees of the little plantation that they had passed on the way up to the cottage that first day. He was also to do a specially good one of another water-wheel, but in quite a different situation, its spindly shape contrasted not with the foliage of trees, but with the swelling curves of the bare downs.

Time was needed for exploring possible future subjects – beyond Furlongs, for instance, some cement works had lately been carved out of the side of the Downs. Peggy took Eric up along a path, from near which they could look down on the whiteness of the exposed chalk walls, of the whitened buildings and engines and the nearby trees and hedges all covered with a fine white powder. Eric was excited by the strangeness of it all – a moon landscape – and they went again up the hill to see it at night, when work went on by the light of flares and arc lamps.

They decided to go and see the manager of the cement works, to ask for his permission to come and paint there. Mr Wilson was surprised but pleased to meet two artists who could see beauty in his works, and said they were welcome to come and draw there; he had been pained to find, when the works were started, that he was considered a desecrator of the countryside and an object of abuse from the local preservationists. (With some reason, of course, and in fact it was realized much later that the white cement dust had been slowly killing the surrounding vegetation, as well as dramatizing its appearance. There are now much stricter regulations.) Eric made a number of paintings there of dolly-engines, of sheds and railway lines and telegraph poles seen against the white chalk walls and backgrounds.

It was also possible from further up that same hill above the cement works to look down on the valley of the Ouse; looking towards Lewes, one could have seen old earth works in the foreground and beyond, the canalized Ouse and patches of flood waters. The Ouse valley is a network of dykes made to control the tidal floods which come right up to Lewes and below the cliff. This was another subject Eric chose.

Exploring in the opposite direction, towards Firle Beacon and Firle village, Eric came on several large greenhouses belonging to an old nurseryman, who as a boy had been on a plant-hunting expedition up the Amazon. Eric enjoyed hearing about this as well as painting pots of cyclamen under a canopy of tomato plants.

Of course, he found subjects nearer home too: Furlongs itself, both interiors and exteriors; the next cottage up the track, known as the Lay; and the immediate surroundings of the Downs; His feelings for them were akin to those described 200 years earlier by Gilbert White, who wrote of the Downs in a letter to a friend and fellow naturalist:

> Though I have now travelled the Sussex-downs upwards of thirty years, yet I still investigate that chain of majestic mountains with fresh admiration year by year, and I think I see new beauties every time I traverse it. The range, which runs from Chichester eastward as far as Eastbourn, is about sixty miles in length, and is called The South Downs, properly speaking, only round Lewes.
>
> For my own part, I think there is somewhat peculiarly sweet and amusing in the shapely figured aspect of chalk-hills, in preference to those of stone, which are rugged, broken, abrupt and shapeless.

It is not surprising that *The Natural History of Selborne* was one of Eric's favourite books, and that he had recommended it so warmly to his students at Eastbourne.

For some time before discovering Furlongs Eric had been feeling that life in London was too distracting and difficult for concentrated work,

Cyclamen and Tomatoes
1935. Watercolour. 18½″
× 23½″. This also
appeared in the 1936
exhibition.
Trustees of the Tate
Gallery, London

and Tirzah too preferred the idea of living in the country. Sharing the holiday house at Great Bardfield had become an occasionally uneasy arrangement; the Bawdens too were wanting to give up living in London and to settle down permanently at Brick House, so Eric and Tirzah had already begun looking at houses in Essex, but had not found anything they liked or that was suitable. They now toyed with the idea of looking for a house in Sussex, so Peggy led them over the Downs, beyond the cement works, to see a derelict farm called Muggery Poke. Eric liked its name and its romantic situation, with views of the distant sea, but it was in a quite uninhabitable condition, and inaccessible except on foot or on horseback, so reluctantly they had to admit it was out of the question.

But when Peggy and Eric were walking home from the cement works, and had just crossed the Newhaven road, they noticed what seemed to be an old track below the side of the lane they were on, and underneath its overgrown vegetation they saw bits of what seemed to be two odd-looking vehicles. They crawled round them but could not make out what they were. When they asked Mr Wilson at the cement works about them, he said they were fever wagons from the Boer War; after the war they had been shipped back to Newhaven. He thought they might have been used by the first prospectors for the cement works and then been dumped where they were now. He had no use for them and offered to sell them for 15 shillings each. Eric liked this idea and the possibility of an independent base of his own on the Downs; there was always the chance of the farmer needing to take his cottage back, and in any case Peggy might not always have room when he wanted to come, so he gladly accepted the offer. There were various arrangements that had to be made; he needed the farmer's permission to bring the caravans to a discreet shelter under some trees at Furlongs; then a breakdown van had to be found to tow them to their carefully planned position, and a carpenter found to make some adjustments to the interiors – all this took time, and it was not till the summer that they were ready.

Long before this, of course, the holidays at Furlongs came to an end and everybody had to go back to London. In fact there had been a good deal of coming and going that spring and summer: Eric had gone off to Colwyn Bay for a week in the middle of April to carry out the decoration of the Tea Room in a new Pier Pavilion which had been built by Professor Adshead to replace that destroyed by fire in 1933. His daughter Mary Adshead (Mrs Stephen Bone), a painter who was also working on the Pavilion, decorating the Auditorium, at the same time, remembers:

> Eric painted all around the stage with marine subjects, shells, seaweed etc. I know that my Father was very pleased with his design, he said that Eric had understood what was wanted and had an architectural sensitivity. The people at Colwyn Bay for whom we were working, had booked Eric and me into a hotel, which turned out to be a sort of holiday home hotel, where parties from Lancashire came for the week – there was a turnaround on Saturday – it was all very matey and lively in a North Country way, with a social host to liven it up in the evenings. I remember Eric and I had a table to ourselves (we must have

Tea at Furlongs 1939. Watercolour, 18" × 22". This was first exhibited at the 1948 Memorial Exhibition under the title of Table laid for Meal, August 1939. R. C. Tuely

seemed fish out of water) and we were greatly amused by our fellow-guests. I know I thought Eric excruciatingly funny at times and very good company; and of course then, as now, I greatly admired his work.

The programme accompanying the Pavilion opening recorded:

Mr. Eric Ravilious strikes an original note in the decoration of the Tea Room. The theme represents a scene on the bed of the ocean. Pink and green seaweeds float through the ruins of a submerged palace. A bright red anchor suggests a connection with the world above. The white and brown arches of the palace are in strong contrast with a golden background. This decorative scheme is in the manner of an eighteenth century scenic wallpaper. The curtains of the Tea Room are shell pink, and the doors and windows grey.

Unfortunately, like most of his mural work, no trace of this survives.

So that she could afford to go to Furlongs for weekends that summer, Peggy managed to get a Saturday morning teaching job at a boys' preparatory school in Seaford, which would pay the fare from London where she was working all the week. Eric had his two days' teaching every other week at the Royal College, and other commissions for engraving or designing kept turning up. One was a screen he was painting for Geoffrey Fry which necessitated a weekend at Oare in June. The Raviliouses also went back to Brick House to continue house hunting. Towards the end of July Eric had to go and help Edward arrange the exhibition of students' work at the college, leaving the glass designs he was busy with for a day or two, while Tirzah was at the Little Gallery pricing the lampshades and waste-paper baskets she had had made with her marbled papers. But Eric went back to Furlongs to paint when he could and by the beginning of August Peggy and the Raviliouses and Percy Horton were back again.

Early in September, Eric and Tirzah had a letter from Edward Bawden telling them about a house to let in Castle Hedingham, a village about ten miles from Great Bardfield. They went back to see it, liked it and took it.

They were soon living in Essex, and Eric found subjects that delighted him there, but he continued to go back to paint at Furlongs when he could. The discoveries made on his first visits had been immensely stimulating and his painting expanded under their influence and moved on to a new stage: in his next one-man show at Zwemmer's early in 1936 half the paintings were of Sussex.

Chapter 7

Bank House was one of a row of small Georgian buildings in the main street of the village of Castle Hedingham, so named because it stood next door to the bank. It had once been a shop with a wide window in the large front room looking on to the street. This room became Eric's studio, with his big work-table in the window. Visitors were struck by its tidiness, with his books and other reference material neatly stored away. It did not look like the accepted idea of an artist's studio, and disappointed his father-in-law. The kitchen, with the scullery beyond, was large enough for Tirzah's marbling as well as the cooking, and there were plenty of rooms upstairs, as the Bank occupied only the ground floor next door; the rest of the building went with Eric and Tirzah's house. There had once been a larger garden at the back, but a diagonal had been cut off it, for which Eric was thankful as, unlike Edward Bawden, he had no instinct for gardening.

The house had needed some redecorating, of course, which the Raviliouses had carried out themselves, but the excitements and exuberances of Brick House were not to be emulated. A sober scheme of plain colour-washed walls, white paint, and Tirzah's marbled wallpapers along the passages and up the staircase made a pleasant background to their life. Friends remember in the dining-room the lithograph of *Midnight Race on the Mississippi*, with its twin-funnelled paddle-steamers, and a collection of china carpet bowls.

The pattern of Eric's life at Hedingham was fluid except for the fixed points of the two days' teaching every other week at the Royal College,

Bank House, Castle Hedingham.

This Essex mill first
appears in a letter from
Eric to Helen Binyon
written from Castle
Hedingham – 'The mill
drawings are going fairly
well and may finish
themselves one day. It is
an extraordinarily
attractive place – a bit
like this. . .' Ravilious
often used ideas more
than once. The mill
features (a) in one of his
1936 engravings of Essex
for Green Line Buses and
again (b) in this undated
wood engraving. It is
interesting to note the use
of the horse in all three
pieces of work.

b

a

and even these could be altered occasionally. The day's activity could be decided by the morning's post. There might be a letter from the Curwen Press, asking for a little engraving to advertize the Southern Railway: 'to strike a Rural and Royal note, maximum joyousness with no colour printing'; a Hamburg hat-shop inquired if Eric were 'an expert artist experienced in drawing hat-stamps for gentlemen's hats'; Green Line Buses wanted some long narrow engravings as an advertisement for Essex Scenery; Bidwell and Bidwell, hairbrush makers, wanted new designs for the backs of their hairbrushes; and so on.

These small jobs, nearly all engravings, always wanted in a hurry, and often having to be altered at a client's whim, could become very tiresome, but on the whole Eric welcomed them. A straightforward statement of what was needed presented him with a small challenge that he enjoyed tackling; there was a satisfaction in 'seeing that the bell should be made to ring'. The variety of the problems, too, gave opportunities for technical experiments, which always interested him. The money earned from these was only a small trickle, but Eric, who by temperament lived entirely in the present, never brooding over the past, or worrying about the future, was not interested in making money, and was content if there were a credit balance in his and Tirzah's joint account.

King George V's Silver Jubilee fell in 1935 and Sunday 5 May was the day chosen for celebrating it. That February Eric was asked to do a job for the Golden Cockerel Press, now in the hands of Christopher Sandford, that he was really pleased about. The book to be illustrated was called *The Hansom Cab and the Pigeons, Being Random Reflections upon the Silver Jubilee of King George V* by L. A. G. Strong.

It was the first time that Ravilious had been asked by that Press to illustrate a book that was not a reprint of a book by a safely out-of-copyright author; and he was delighted to be asked to illustrate a book concerned with the present day. Although the job needed to be ready in a fortnight, he accepted it with enthusiasm, and finished it on time.

For the frontispiece he engraved a broken-down hansom cab, with pigeons resting in it or flying between it and their dove-cot. The sun is shining through the leafy trees behind. The other designs are all smaller, decorations rather than illustrations, and are full of life and movement.

When, early in March, Eric arrived at the college for one of his teaching days, he found great excitement in the staffroom about plans for the Silver Jubilee street decorations. Rothenstein was a member of the committee appointed to decide on these. To begin with, his idea was to have triumphal arches at the entrance to the city, but it was objected that these might interfere with traffic arrangements; Rothenstein then suggested a transformation of the unprepossessing railway bridges under which the royal procession would be moving. This plan was accepted, and it was decided that the Royal College students should decorate the Ludgate Hill bridge, while the Slade students tackled the bridge on the Embankment.

Ravilious noted that for the students this was a competition for honour and glory alone:

These things are never paid – Rothenstein wants something baroque (pronounced by him, *barr*ock) and mighty fanciful, so everyone is designing a bridge like a pantomime scene, with Neptunes and mermaids and Britannias – I'm not sure that it really is a good idea when

Frontispiece engraved by Ravilious for *The Hansom Cab and The Pigeons* by L. A. G. Strong (The Golden Cockerel Press, 1935). There was a limited edition of 212 numbered copies signed by the author, and 1000 unnumbered and unsigned copies.

you have to compete with BOVRIL ten foot high – John Nash (newly appointed to the College) wants to use sheets of tin, and I should like scaffolding with no paint and lots of flags – but the baroque idea will win probably. [It did].

But it was not the official decorations of the main streets, nor even Barnett Freedman's specially designed and outsized 1½d postage stamp that were the most attractive features of the Jubilee celebrations. It was the decorations put up on their own houses and along their own streets by the inhabitants of the little streets of towns and villages all over the country that best expressed the general rejoicing. It was a real flowering of popular art.

At Castle Hedingham, the shop's supply of flags had seemed bountiful, but when Eric and Tirzah went to buy the triangular pennons they had particularly liked, they found they had all been sold. So Tirzah made some herself, superior ones of shirting and yellow satin, to be strung up and stretched round the house and railings, with the help of their weekend visitors, Robert Wellington, J. M. Richards and Peggy Angus. The weather for Jubilee Sunday was ideal, and conditions perfect for the bonfire and fireworks in the evening; the village really gave itself up to the general abandon and cheerfulness: in such a quiet place the effect was almost disturbing.

When Eric and Tirzah first arrived at Castle Hedingham they did not know anyone else living in the village, but they were to make great friends with two young couples who came to live there soon after their own arrival. The first pair that they got to know were the new young vicar and his wife, Guy and Evelyn Hepher. The first time that Eric called at their large old Georgian vicarage, he found the vicar having a bonfire of the temperance hymnbooks inherited from his predecessor – an activity that Eric certainly approved of. The vicarage was too large and uncomfortable to be easily run, but it afforded a refuge to the Raviliouses one very cold Christmas when all their pipes had frozen up. Eric made a good painting of the outside in a snowstorm that same winter.

The Hephers had a little boy called David, who was to become the playmate of Eric and Tirzah's own new baby son, John, born that June. One of the reasons for the Bawdens and Raviliouses deciding to leave London was that they thought the country a better place for bringing up a family, and both Charlotte and Tirzah felt the time had come to do this: Charlotte's baby, a little girl they called Joanna, had been born in February.

The other young couple who came to live in Hedingham were an architect and his wife called Robert and Kay Gooden. Their house was quite close to Bank House, and the four of them often spent the evening together, playing dominoes, listening to records or visiting the little local cinema. Kay Gooden had read English at Somerville and Eric enjoyed meeting someone who kept up with all the new books, and could sometimes lend them. One evening he came home with H. G. Wells' *Autobiography*, and the life of Nijinsky by his wife. These were the sort of books he most enjoyed. Boswell's *Dr Johnson* was another, and one that he once took for company on a long painting holiday. When *Kilvert's Diary* came out in 1940, he was enchanted by it. For fun he read P. G. Wodehouse.

The only thing Eric missed in Hedingham was the atmosphere of work – 'work' always meant 'art in the making' to him. For this he had to go over to Brick House, but Great Bardfield was within cycling distance, and Eric and Edward were able to go on exchanging ideas and showing their watercolours to each other as they felt the need.

On the whole it was a quiet, hard-working life in Hedingham, and after a day's engraving 'crawling like a fly over all these finicky bits of wood' Eric felt a need for gossipy company and noise and some sort of activity. They lived opposite The Bell, and Eric liked to go and play pub games there, taking with him any visitor they had staying.

From time to time there were social excitements. At Whitsun they went to a splendid party at Brick House, where they found the artist Robert Medley and the dancer Rupert Doone being shown round the garden. The next arrivals were the Harold Curwens of the Curwen Press and his

Vicarage in Winter
9 January 1935.
Watercolour. 18" × 22".
This was exhibited at
Zwemmer's in 1936 and
has appeared in all
subsequent exhibitions of
Ravilious's work.
Mrs Guy Hepher

two children, followed by Bowk Sinclair, her brother, and John Aldridge. Delicious party food for everyone had been prepared with artistry by Charlotte.

On Whit Monday, there was the cricket match between the village and an eleven, which included Eric, playing for the Double Crown Club. This was a Dining Club founded in 1924 by Oliver Simon and Hubert Foss. There were forty founder members, all men passionately and professionally interested in the making of books, and in exchanging views about what they were hoping to achieve. The club met between four and six times a year. Members were invited in turn to design and print the menu, which would be criticized and judged by the president, after which a paper would be read, followed by a discussion.

Eric had undertaken to do the cover of the menu for the forty-ninth dinner at the club at the Café Royal in May 1935. He had made a handsome engraving more or less illustrating the dishes on the bill of fare, with the spotted side of the sole in the middle used as a ground for the white engraved lettering (all engraved lettering had to be cut in reverse, of course).

The Double Crown Club cricket team was captained by Francis Meynell, and here is Eric's description of the match:

It was a holiday playing cricket yesterday, only the game went on a bit too long for my liking and I began to get a little absent-minded in the deep field after tea. However I was not out, hit four balls and made one run. I also bowled a few overs and in consequence feel stiff as a poker to-day. Poor Oliver Simon made a duck, out first ball. The Stracheys did best – one I don't know hit up 68, but all the same the village was too good for us and won comfortably. It all felt just like being back at school, especially the trestle tea with slabs of bread and butter, and that wicked-looking cheap cake; also there were the identical speeches from the captains. I enjoyed it all very much, and shall hope to play again, as Meynell kindly said that my bowling was of erratic length but promising and I should have been put on before. Think of the honour and glory there.

Offers of work of various kinds kept coming along. The Golden Cockerel Press asked him to illustrate a Russian poem, but Eric considered it was 'badly translated doggerel, rather like the Pied Piper in subject', and turned the proposal down. He suggested instead, as something he would like to do, a picture book of shops. This was an idea that had been simmering in his mind lately, and at first he thought the book might be an alphabet of shops. He had just been enjoying painting the interior of the Hedingham butcher's shop which would be good for the letter B. The Golden Cockerel did not reject this idea altogether, but the project hung fire for a time and no decision was made.

Then in June Ravilious had an unexpected letter from a fellow artist called Tom Hennell, asking if he would like to do some illustrations for his new verses. It was not a commission, but Hennell felt his poems might appeal more to a publisher if accompanied by Ravilious engravings; then if they were accepted, the takings could be shared between them.

Tom Hennell's first meeting with Ravilious and Bawden had been in the Brick House kitchen one day before breakfast. He was bicycling on

Menu for the Double Crown Club with visual references to Hors d'oevre variés, Melon frappé, Filet de Sole Royal, Supreme de Volaille Alsacienne, Les Asperges de Lauris and Quartier de Poire au vin rouge.

One of the four engravings on wood by Eric Ravilious for **Poems by Thomas Hennell** *(Oxford University Press, 1936). This engraving, facing the poem 'Scenes of the Sower's Parable', is taken from one of the limited edition of 50, printed on Basingwerk Parchment and signed by the author and artist.*

his way to see friends in Suffolk and Norfolk, and had asked the inhabitant of the other half of Brick House for a lodging for the night; she had told him he could wash in the kitchen. In fact this was the start of a friendship between all three artists. Tom Hennell, once accurately described by Eric as of Graeco-Roman appearance, was a watercolourist, and the unworldly son of a parson and was himself a lay preacher; he was passionately interested in all country creatures and country crafts, as his rather uneven poems proclaim.

Eric decided he would like to make engravings for the book and proposed doing four. These he did that summer and Hennell when he saw them told Eric he thought them exquisite. The book was published the following year by the Oxford University Press, but sadly it made no impact on the public and was remaindered in 1940.

When there was a lull in jobs arriving, Eric took the chance to explore the neighbourhood for painting subjects. If there were some dramatic change in the look of the country – floods perhaps, or snow, or just a marvellous day – all other work would be abandoned and a painting started. Except for a few surprising places that he discovered, he found it difficult to find country that didn't remind him of other people's paintings – 'compositions with all the ingredients'. But there had been the junk yard where enormous black-faced sheep ran about the place, jumping over pans and corrugated iron with a beautiful agility and a great deal of clatter, while he was drawing the derelict hansom cab; and he was a good deal excited by a pig farm. He liked everything about a pig, except its eye – and the barn he found them in had an intricate cage of beams, making a perfect background for the pigs. The ones in the part of the barn where he was drawing were very subdued all that day, having only that morning been gelded. He was thankful to have arrived just as the thirty-eighth and last pig was finished.

The December snow only lasted an hour when it came, but Eric managed to do a drawing, most of it from memory, and to enjoy scratching the snow spots all over the drawing with a penknife. He explored further afield, too, to a white Hovis mill, and to the polo-ball factory at Halstead and the Tiptree greenhouses. He had lately been experimenting with some new watercolour paints: Mars orange, Rubens red, and brown madder. He always bought whole pans of paint at Newman's shop in Soho Square, an artists' colourman that had been grinding and mixing paints for at least a century, and universally believed to be the best. Newman's was destroyed during the war.

After Eric's first successful show at Zwemmer's, Robert Wellington had said that they should aim at having a show at least every three years. He also expected to be able to sell a few paintings throughout the year, so he needed always to have some in stock in the gallery, with Eric, if possible, supplying a new one every other month. The one-man shows at the Zwemmer Gallery could not be on for as long as a month, so that representatives of the further away provincial galleries, valuable patrons as they were, were not always able to get to shows in time. Against this, Wellington stressed the importance of keeping enough paintings back to make an impressive second show. He offered to have this at his gallery in October or November of 1935, or in the following spring. It was actually held in early February 1936.

It must be remembered that Eric reckoned that not more than one out of two or three of his paintings was likely to be successful, and he tore up those that he felt were not.

Eric had also been back to Furlongs to paint several times during the year, and when Edward Bawden went over to Hedingham to see Eric's latest watercolours, he liked the new Sussex ones best. Earlier in the summer Edward had suggested going to draw at Harwich with Eric, but when they went to look round it, they didn't like it enough, and planned instead to go again to Newhaven, and stay at the Hope Inn. They would go at the beginning of August, after they had put up the end-of-year students' exhibition in the design room at the college.

On the way to Newhaven, Eric and Tirzah and the baby John went to

Village Street
Watercolour. 15³⁄₄″ ×
20¹⁄₄″. This view of
Castle Hedingham is one
of Ravilious's rare
peopled pictures. But, as is
common in his work, the
faces are featureless.
Towner Art Gallery,
Eastbourne

Eric's parents at the window with their canary.

Eastbourne to stay with the Garwood family for a celebration dinner in honour of the first grandchild; then Eric went to stay with his elderly parents on the other side of Eastbourne. In spite of his rather strange boyhood, Eric had nearly always managed to stay on good terms with his father. They too were delighted with the baby when Tirzah brought him to meet them; he had a look of Eric, though blue-eyed and fair.

Eric spent some of his time at his parents' home finishing the engravings for Hennell's book. He has described his parents' canary as:

sitting on my left-hand while I am engraving, and watching the chips fly – I have to shoo him off the block sometimes. He sits very quietly on my shoulder as long as he is allowed, but makes rather a mess of my coat, so I can't encourage him too much. His whistle in my ear is so startling if he begins to sing. He hates people with hats on, hopping about the room and chirping until they take them off.

Directly Eric got to Newhaven, a terrific storm blew up, the worst for years. He walked to the end of the jetty to look at the lighthouse: 'The spray from the breakers crashing on the weather-side of the breakwater was a quite extraordinary sight – I got very wet and think now it was almost a dangerous walk out there, but worth it. The scene was like one of those extravagant and formless pictures of Turner's.' Edward arrived the next day, and they stayed a week, and painted intensively all the time.

When Robert Wellington had written about the dates for the next show, he also mentioned a scheme he was busy planning. Its aim was to introduce the work of living artists to school children. Many schools bought modern colour reproductions of historic masters of European painting,

Channel Steamer 1935. Watercolour. 20½" × 17¾". Probably exhibited in 1936 as **Channel Steamer Leaving Harbour**, this painting of the Newhaven boat was one of the three borrowed by the Tate Gallery to exhibit at the New York World's Fair in 1939. Estate of the late Helen Binyon

*Newhaven Harbour 1937 Ravilious's 'Homage to Seurat', one of the series 'Lithographs for Schools' (Contemporary Lithographs). The **New Statesman** said 'The first series of ten is extremely promising. There is something in fact for every sort of taste except bad taste....'*

but he felt that children should have the chance to become familiar with the art of their own day. Education officers, particularly Henry Morris, and the pioneer teacher of 'child art', Marion Richardson, were consulted. They agreed that the first idea of getting artists to paint murals in schools would cost far too much, and decided that the best plan would be to invite some chosen artists each to make a colour lithograph, drawing them direct on to the prepared stones, one for each colour, at the Curwen Press, and thus make original works of art that the schools could afford.

Eventually a company called Contemporary Lithographs with two directors, Robert Wellington and the artist John Piper, was formed to organize the making and the marketing of the prints. The ten artists they chose for the first series were Edward Bawden, Barnett Freedman, Clive Gardiner, Norah McGuinness, Robert Medley, John Nash, Paul Nash, Eric Ravilious, Graham Sutherland and H. S. Williamson. They were to choose their own subjects, which would aim at appealing to one of two age groups, four to five, or eight to nine. The size of each print was to be 20 × 30 inches.

Eric chose for his subject Newhaven Harbour. The whole scene has a sensitive clarity and a beautiful luminosity. But it is a completely uninhabited one; there is not even a little dog sniffing about its tidy cleanness. Eric's own title for it was 'Homage to Seurat'.

The lithographs were on sale to the public as well as to the schools, but at the slightly higher price of £1 11s 6d a print. It was a slow job getting them all drawn and printed, and they were not published until 1937.

For Eric this introduction to the craft of lithography was the opening of a door. It must have been a great release to work with colour, after so

much black and white engraving, and his experience of painting in transparent watercolours would have been an invaluable guide in his new experiments with lithographic inks and chalks.

His idea for the book of shops which he had offered to the Golden Cockerel Press was now, after some delay, accepted by Christopher Sandford but on the condition that it would have to be a speculation on Eric's part; there would be a 20% royalty, but no fee. There were rather long, drawn-out discussions, and the possibility of sharing expenses with another publisher considered, but after his days of work at the Curwen Press, learning about lithography, Eric had become excited about the idea of doing his illustrations as lithographs. He suggested this to the Golden Cockerel, but they eventually decided against it.

Noel Carrington, the publisher of Country Life Books, had lately asked Eric to do the illustrations for a new gardening book and had sent him the manuscript to look at. But Eric felt that as gardening was not his line, he could not do such a big job without being really interested. So a little later, when the discussions with Christopher Sandford came to nothing, Eric offered his shops to Noel Carrington, who was very interested in the idea. They met in London and the scheme was settled. For the next year or so, Eric worked on and off on the shops, tracking each one down, and making notes and drawings.

While he was still thinking of an alaphabet providing a thread to hang his shops on, he had made an experimental lithograph for G, founded on the greenhouse at Firle, but the alphabet was soon abandoned, and indeed was not necessary. It was just a question of noticing shops that particularly attracted or amused him. He enjoyed the treasure-hunt of looking for them, and had already found a Soho bread shop, a funeral furnisher and Buzzard's Cake Department. In the end there were twenty-four shops, but he had to wait some time before the lithographs could be drawn, and the book did not appear until 1938.

In November 1935 a new periodical was launched by Oliver Simon of the Curwen Press. It was a quadrimestrial of typography and graphic

*Cover design for Number 6 of the **Curwen Newsletter** c1936. Engraved on wood.*

*This beautiful design for the Prospectus of **The Cornhill** magazine was commissioned by John Murray, 1933.*

*Title page for **Winters of Content** by Osbert Sitwell (Duckworth, 1932). Engraved on wood.*

arts, and was called *Signature*.

The first number contained three well-illustrated articles: 'A Sanctuary of Printing: The Record Room at the University Press, Oxford', by Holbrook Jackson; 'New Draughtsmen', by Paul Nash; and 'The Printed and Published Wood-Engravings of Eric Ravilious'. There were also some book reviews, and a new alphabet of initial letters, designed by Barnett Freedman for the Baynard Press, printed in red and black. Among the advertisements on the last page is the name of the Kynoch Press printed in the letters of an alphabet designed and cut by Eric.

There was a short foreword to the Ravilious article, followed by the impressive list of the printed and published wood engravings of Eric Ravilious, grouped under the headings of books, prospectuses, designs for book jackets and miscellaneous, engraved between 1926 and 1935.

The eight pages of illlustrations that follow were chosen, as the editor explains, from Ravilious's less accessible work; those that made for business and miscellaneous purposes, rather than his better known engravings for the private presses, and particularly the Golden Cockerel Press. The variety of designs he selected, Oliver Simon thought, 'would rank amongst his finest and most spontaneous achievements'.

It is interesting to see the development of Eric's work in the gathering together of nine years of wood engraving, the growing sureness of design matched by greater sureness of technique. Of the many engravings illustrated especially striking is an abstract design of an exploding star, for the cover of Number 6 of the *Curwen Newsletter*. There is a beautiful design for a prospectus of *The Cornhill* magazine, a sheaf of corn standing up between the sun and the moon, and a handsome formal design of a view down a Renaissance street for the title page of *Winters of Content* by Osbert Sitwell. All the engravings sparkle with vitality and have the unmistakable Ravilious hallmark.

This gathering together, this adding up of the sum of Ravilious's engravings so far, happened to mark the peak of his output. He still went on developing as an engraver, and produced some more fine work, but he began to accept fewer commissions for this, as other forms of applied design engaged his inventiveness. Of these the two most important were pottery and lithography.

His work for the firm of Josiah Wedgwood will be described in the next chapter, but before we leave 1935, we must remember that if this was the year of a Silver Jubilee in England, in Germany it was the year that Hitler, who had been in power since 1933, introduced conscription, and in Italy the year that Mussolini invaded Abyssinia.

Even artists so busily and so rightly absorbed in their own work as Eric Ravilious, and with no instinctive interest in politics, could not help hearing the distant warnings. '*The Statesman* gets more depressing each week . . . the thought of another war is unbearable', he wrote in May of this year.

For the next four years, of course, the warnings were to get louder and louder.

Chapter 8

Soon after Eric and Tirzah had left London and gone to live at Castle Hedingham, Eric wrote to Cecilia Dunbar Kilburn to thank her for her present of a blue rug for their new house. He went on to tell her that:

> Gwyneth Lloyd Thomas was over to tea last week. She had heard – from the Bowk of course – that you were going to China and I think taking Mrs Hay and me – I'm not quite sure of Mrs Hay but she was mentioned – a cheerful, reckless, inaccurate Bowker I feel sure, but stranger things *have* happened. At the moment we have £12 in the Bank . . . so that a small miracle would need to happen if I am to go as far as that. Perhaps it will. But I am hanged if I know that really and truly I want to go; as an idea I feel very much attracted. I imagine myself painting the most alluring hill country in terre verte and grey, untroubled by anything whatever – that is why I should like to go I think.

The explanation of the rumour that had reached Eric was that Cecilia had been invited to visit a friend of hers then living in Peking. After her three visits to India and Burma, she was dallying with the delightful idea of going to China, and thinking of persuading some friends to come with her, when a quite different possibility cropped up. The new registrar at the Royal College of Art, Athole Hay (Hubert Wellington having been appointed principal of the Edinburgh College of Art) had now asked Cecilia to join him as partner in a new project for a shop 'for the sale of objects of applied art'. While still at college, Cecilia had once vaguely thought of some day opening a picture gallery to help young painters, and she felt much drawn to the new scheme. Visions of China faded; directors were found and plans for the new shop, which was to be called Dunbar Hay, were made. Eventually it was opened in premises at 15 Albemarle Street, with Cecilia installed as manager and, for a time, Jennifer Fry as her assistant.

A printed letter had first been sent out to suitable artists, which began:

> It is proposed to open in the near future a shop for the sale of objects of applied art which in the ordinary way might be difficult to market.
>
> Every year a great deal of excellent work is done which falls into obscurity between gallery and shop. The gallery is altogether too formidable; the ordinary shop is too commercial and wants quantity for cheapness.

It might seem from this that Dunbar Hay's aim was to be a second Little Gallery, and when Miss Rose heard of the new shop, she was much disconcerted at the idea of this new rival to her own so carefully and successfully built-up craft shop – might not its novelty lure away her own special customers?

There was some overlapping, of course, but in fact the shops were rather different in aim, and in what they sold. Miss Rose was guided by her personal taste in excellence, and would not sell anything she did not like herself, and hardly ever anything not made by the hands of a skilled craftsman. Dunbar Hay had the aim of finding and selling the best of its kind, whether hand- or machine-made. This meant Cecilia had to visit textile and other factories, for instance, and discover what the manufacturers were producing. She would have liked to keep to English goods, but found the furnishing fabrics she was shown so dull in colour that she had to order from France as well. There was Swedish glass on sale too.

From the first, Eric was asked to design for Dunbar Hay and was paid a small retaining fee. Before the shop opened, he designed a chair for them. Four chairs were eventually made in unstained mahogany, inlaid with boxwood, and with seat cushions covered with one of Enid Marx's printed stuffs. He engraved a delightful design for the trade-card, which shows the façade of a doll's house shop. Displayed in the shop window, with amusing distortions of scale, are spoons and forks as big as an armchair, a large round teapot floating above a small round table, and a length of material unrolling from ceiling to floor. On two oval trays are engraved the words 'China, Glass, Interior Decorations and Furniture'. But the chief work of Eric's that Dunbar Hay sold was the pottery made by the firm of Josiah Wedgwood and decorated with Ravilious designs.

In 1935 Ravilious had been summoned to meet the head of the firm, also called Josiah Wedgwood, to discuss the possibility of doing some work for them. He agreed to make some trial designs which would be suitable for reproduction by the eighteenth-and nineteenth-century traditional English method of transfer-printing, whereby patterns printed on paper from engraved copper plates are transferred to porcelain or pottery and then fired, the paper disappearing in the firing.

On 17 July 1936, Eric went up to Stoke-on-Trent to stay for a night or two, and to see the works, and show Josiah Wedgwood some designs for plates and a special mug to celebrate the coronation of King Edward VIII. The king's father, George V, had not lived long after his Jubilee the year before, and had died at the end of January 1936. Eric described the drawing for the coronation mug as having 'a submerged royal arms with the heads of the royal beasts sticking out into the fireworks above'. The letters E and R were on either side of the coat of arms, and on the other side of the mug the date of 1937. On the top half of the mug exploding fireworks are drawn in black with yellow accents here and there, and the lower half has a light blue band of a transparent colour all round. The whole mug is gay, the lettering and figures just the right weight, and all the elements happily balanced. Its design pleased Josiah Wedgwood and they decided to produce it as quickly as possible, as well as most of the other designs for tableware.

It was an exciting visit for Ravilious. The first day had been taken up by looking all over the factory, and he had found it exhausting having to talk to so many people. The next day, as he wrote in a letter:

> This afternoon, I'm going to the works again to have a look at the museum and make a few experiments. I am sorry to say that the [Wedgwood] family think my beautiful designs above the heads of their public and that to begin with something should be done that is safer and more understandable. I argued about this most of the afternoon. The argument is whether to alter the present way of doing things in a

Two chairs from the set
designed for Dunbar Hay
by Ravilious. Unstained
mahogany inlaid with
boxwood.
Cecilia, Lady Sempill.

Dunbar Hay Ltd

China
Glass

Interior
Decorations
Furniture

15 Albemarle St.
London W.1.
Telephone
Regent 3522

The Dunbar Hay trade
card. This was printed in
two colours – black and
buff.
Cecilia, Lady Sempill.

Wedgwood pattern book entry for Ravilious's design for a mug 'to commemorate the Coronation of their Majesties King George VI, Queen Elizabeth, 1937.'
Trustees of the Wedgwood Museum, Barlaston, Staffordshire

hurry or to attempt it by degrees. I was for a clean sweep and they want a method of slow percolation: it all means that I had better think of some new designs – something if possible that suits all the markets at once, so I must go back and see if I am clever enough to do this.

The Coronation mug will be produced which is something; but you should see the one Laura Knight has designed – bloody beyond description – The Wedgwoods say how bad the thing is, but point out how big the sales will be – I wish her well but it seems a pity.

Old Josiah's own patterns are the most perfect pottery designs I've seen and they moulder here because they haven't the wide appeal either – I believe we are the only designers the firm have had, and it is a pity I can't raise up his ghost to help along my argument. Dame L. K. must be giving him a turn just now.

However, a little later he was writing about the new pottery designs:

All that this job needs is tactful persuasion and some propaganda in the London shops. I feel now that it won't really be the lost cause my letter suggested. But it will need far more time and patience than I thought necessary at first, and visits to Stoke every month or so. I must either give up the job or do it pretty thoroughly, and with a tactful bullying of the Wedgwood family and their travellers. At the moment, their factory could be doing good pottery and they seem to be too timid to give it a trial.

He went up to Stoke again in October, this time with Cecilia and a friend of hers, who owned a powerful car and drove the three of them. Cecilia, representing Dunbar Hay, did some preaching and propaganda – 'she laid about her and spoke her mind'. The coronation mug was finished; it looked bigger than Eric expected, but 'he liked a mantelpiece ornament [which it really was] pretty big'. 'It is a change' (one of Eric's key words of approval) 'and I like it and felt almost excited when they brought it out.'

The coronation mug was produced in time for Christmas; the first London shop to have it on sale was Dunbar Hay. The first customer to buy one was Mrs Simpson!

The mug was the first piece of pottery to be produced for Wedgwood but a dinner service called 'Persephone' was soon in production. Its design had been inspired by some drawings Eric had made some months earlier of the Harvest Festival in Hedingham Church. It was followed by another

Four Wedgwood Queen's Ware mugs all bearing designs by Ravilious: **top** *'Barlaston Mug' designed in 1939 and put into production in 1940 to commemorate the move from Etruria to Barlaston;* **right** *the 'Coronation mug in blue was designed in anticipation of the Coronation of Edward VIII, and was later adapted in green for the Coronation of George VI; the 'Alphabet' mug designed in 1937. Trustees of the Wedgwood Museum, Barlaston, Staffordshire*

mug with an alphabet design – a whole nursery set was developed from this – and, of course, after the abdication a new coronation mug had to be produced.

Eric had to limit his designs to shapes provided for him by Keith Murray, an architect who designed all the Wedgwood forms, as well as the new factory just being built. In February, Eric wrote to raise the question of the weight and thickness of plates sent to him as samples, and had this answer from Wedgwood:

> It is just possible that these were abnormally thick, but if your criticism applies to the general run of the concave plates you have seen at Etruria, I am afraid we cannot alter it. The weight and thickness of the concave plate has been arrived at as a compromise between the ideally thin plate as originally made and as seen in the Museum today, and a thick unbreakable plate as sometimes asked for by the trade. I am afraid it would be an impossible complication to run a special stock of light plates for your patterns, and further, if we did this, they would probably be criticized as being too thin and fragile for use.

It was this kind of compromise which Eric found so hampering. But Wedgwood were very pleased with his designs: the next year they were thanking him for his complete set of drawings for his Travel and Garden Patterns. 'Speaking for myself', Tom Wedgwood wrote, 'I am delighted with them, particularly the Garden Pattern; you must have put in a tremendous lot of work on these patterns since you were down here, and I do think you are to be congratulated on the result.'

The general rule seems to have been for Eric to make a number of suggestions and designs each year, of which one or two would be carried out. In time, he sadly realized that those he thought the least interesting were always the ones to be chosen. For instance, there were some designs

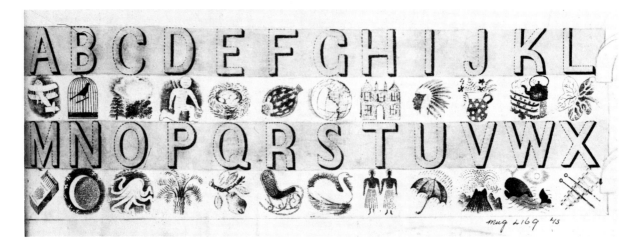

Wedgwood pattern book entry for the 'Alphabet' mug c1937. Trustees of the Wedgwood Museum, Barlaston, Staffordshire

for cups and saucers with thin white patterns on solid dark grounds which Miss Rose remembers seeing at the Little Gallery and thinking lovely, but which were never used and seem to have disappeared at Wedgwood.

On the whole, Eric enjoyed the demands for designs, and there might have been really large sales, especially in America, had it not been for the war. The one he got most excited about was for a Boat Race Bowl, of a shape called a Harvard Bowl, or alternatively a Burslem Vase – the same design would fit either shape. With Eric's own memories of Hammersmith Bridge and the Boat Race to inspire him, he had great fun working out the design and passing on the excitements he remembered. Tom Wedgwood felt that there should be a scene inside the bowl, and suggested 'Boat Race Night'. This was provided to Wedgwood's – and Eric's – satisfaction. All his designs were carried out in earthenware, except for one china tea set.

The arrangement with Wedgwood was for Eric to work six weeks in the year for them and 'although I don't know quite what the fee will be,' he wrote, 'it is something beautifully disproportionate to the time and effort and I'll be able to live for six weeks like a coloured boxer.' Eric always had this unworldly attitude to money, and he marvelled at, but did not, I think, envy his old college friend, Barnett Freedman, when they met in London and he was told by Barnett that he now had a kind of retaining fee from a millionaire just to paint pictures, and so was above the necessity of exhibiting them. The B.B.C. poster Barnett Freedman had just been commissioned to do had only taken him a day and had made £105.

This same carefree attitude of Eric's was shown in the first days of the war when he told Cecilia Dunbar Kilburn that he had written to Wedgwood offering to resign, as it was quite useless trying to go on to designing for them now, and 'was given the sack gratefully'.

Eric was becoming more determined in his aim to do more serious work and fewer little jobs, which the new Wedgwood assignments would only further. So, when Athole Hay wrote and asked him to take on some more teaching at the Royal College, he decided against it. In fact, a year later Eric gave up teaching altogether, both at the college, and the Ruskin School at Oxford.

He had chiefly objected to his teaching days as an interruption and

Above *Wedgwood Queen's Ware in the 'Travel' series, designed by Ravilious c1938.*

Below *A plate and the original watercolour for one of the 'Travel' series vignettes. Although designed by Ravilious before World War II, it was not put into production until c1953. Trustees of the Wedgwood Museum, Barlaston, Staffordshire*

grudged the time away from his own work, but his students at the college seem to have valued his help. Here is what one of them, John O'Connor, the painter and wood engraver, has written about him as a teacher:

Ravilious clearly did not enjoy his instruction days and often passed through them in a bored way; but immediately his interest was aroused, all the latent vitality he had would come out in enthusiastic talk and suggestions to a student or students. He passed quickly by the routine work and used to be happy to settle on some piece of engraving, or mural work, or a piece of fabric printing for the best part of an hour at a time.

Geoffrey Wales, another gifted student of that time, wrote:

We were very fond of Ravilious as a teacher and admired his work very much. As an engraver, I chiefly remember his concern with tone. Upon one occasion, he said that if one had a design in which there were three horses, one black, one white and one grey, one should arrange them as follows: The black horse against the light sky, the white against a black tree and the grey against either the dark or light areas. It was at this time that he was designing covers for a series of London Transport booklets, dealing with country walks. They are still in print [in 1975] and show the point he was making very clearly.

Geoffrey Wales continued:

My wife, who was also a student at the Royal College of Art, remembers him taking a party of students round the Victoria and Albert Museum, and emphasizing, after looking with them at a widely different group of objects, how important it was to be able to enjoy as many differing things as possible.

In 1936, John O'Connor and I helped Ravilious to decorate one of the R.C.A. studios, which was used as a team room on Diploma Day. We covered the walls and ceiling with yards and yards of butter muslin, at sixpence per yard, and quite transformed the room, so that it took on the elegance which one always associated with Ravilious.

Diploma Day, held in the Lecture Theatre of the Victoria and Albert Museum at the end of the summer term, was always a formal occasion. On this Diploma Day in 1936, just before the proceedings began, Ravilious came in from the door on the right, walked slowly along between the rows of chairs waiting for the staff on the platform, but instead of sitting down, he just kept on walking until he had gone through the door on the other side, leaving the ceremony behind. 'That was a neat get-away, sir,' one of his students said to him afterwards. It was a characteristic impulse, almost a surrealist gesture.

In fact it was in 1936 that the first big international surrealist exhibition burst upon London. Its ideas were too revolutionary to be understood at once; some visitors were very excited by what they saw, some very shocked and indignant, but most were probably just baffled. It was held in June in the large New Burlington Galleries, Burlington Gardens, and showed works by fifty-eight different artists, eighteen of them English. The exhibition had been organized by small committees from the five countries taking part. Under the chairmanship of Rupert Lee, the English committee consisted of Hugh Sykes Davies, David Gascoyne, Humphrey Jennings, E. McKnight Kauffer, Henry Moore, Paul Nash, Roland Penrose and Herbert Read. There was a catalogue of the exhibition with a preface by André Breton and an introduction by Herbert Read, who wrote of 'superrealism' rather than 'surrealism' and reminded his readers that England had already produced two 'superrealists' in William Blake and Lewis Carroll.

Since 1928, Paul Nash's paintings, and indeed his remarkable photo-

Wedgwood Queen's Ware 'Burslem Vase' and 'Harvard Bowl' featuring the famous 'Boat Race Day' design, with a Mermaid device inside the vase; the bowl interior shows Piccadilly Circus on Boat Race Night. Originally designed c1938. **Below** *Another scene on the 'Boat Race' bowl.* Trustees of the Wedgwood Museum, Barlaston, Staffordshire

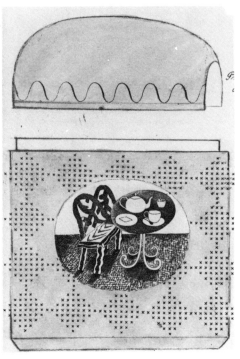

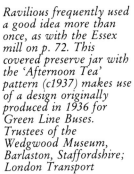

Ravilious frequently used a good idea more than once, as with the Essex mill on p. 72. This covered preserve jar with the 'Afternoon Tea' pattern (c1937) makes use of a design originally produced in 1936 for Green Line Buses. Trustees of the Wedgwood Museum, Barlaston, Staffordshire; London Transport

graphs, had reflected his own excitement about the ideas of the surrealist painters, and he had initiated a surrealist group. At the time of the exhibition, he was sending messages to the college through his brother John, that the R.C.A. should be paying more attention to surrealism. There does not seem to have been an immediate response. Ravilious was never much interested in theories about art and kept aloof from movements. He occasionally found his own dreams or nightmares worth writing down, but was no more interested in Freud's theories – though perhaps he was a little scared of them – than in other theories, aesthetic or political. Percy Horton, now in charge of life-drawing classes at the college, had been reading about surrealism with intense disapproval and thought 'it was damned cheek of André Breton and Co. to pose as Marxists'. As for John Nash, he was as unresponsive as Ravilious; a year or two later he was writing this from the Pembrokeshire coast where he was painting:

> Llangereth beach here would be a happy hunting-ground for the surrealist – so many 'objects' there, lost and wanting to be found or 'trouvés', and waiting to lose themselves again, or just *there* hardly needing looking for – I succumbed to the fever and drew a few treetrunks. I know they looked like cast-up sea monsters – childish, isn't it?

In the next summer of 1937, there was to be held in Paris one of those huge international exhibitions at which different nations are invited to put up a pavilion, whose design and contents have been chosen to express the ideas about its country that the government of the day wishes to emphasise.

The foreword that was written for the *Guide to the British Pavilion* gives a very clear idea of the image that the Council for Art and Industry chose for Britain:

The Paris Exhibition of 1937 is concerned with the arts and crafts in modern life, the arts and crafts of industry (between art and craft there can be no true distinction). H. M. Government in the United Kingdom have agreed to participate, and at their invitation the Council for Art and Industry (appointed by the Board of Trade) have undertaken responsibility for the design of the Government Pavilion and for the selection and display of all that is to be shown in it.

The Council for Art and Industry have decided to attempt to picture to the world those elements of the current civilisation of Western Europe which had been contributed mainly by Great Britain. As an index to these elements, it is only necessary to pass in review those English words which have found their place in the French language: e.g., Sport = le sport; Weekend = le weekend; Tennis = le tennis; Football = le football; Golf = le golf; Five o'clock tea = le fiv' oclock; Bridge = le bridge; Picnic = le picnic. Some people, maybe, will feel it unfortunate that the list relates so much to pleasure rather than to work! Yet it is certain that no civilized life is possible which does not, as part of its business and justification, aim at enjoyment.

And so, in our Pavilion, our sports and games are well illustrated. Our week-end cottage and our love of the sea and of the countryside receive conspicuous treatment; and so far as industry is concerned, only those things which relate to our persons and our homes are collected together – our dress, our tableware, pottery, glass and our furniture. In the selection of these things the English tradition of sound construction and good workmanship has been kept in the forefront, and in design the particularly English quality has been sought.

Ravilious photographed by Norman Parkinson sitting in front of a model of his 'Tennis' exhibit designed for the Sports section of the British Pavilion, Paris Exhibition 1937.

This image of an England largely rural and inhabited by comfortably off sportsmen struck many English visitors as misleadingly out-of-date and trivial, though the displays were pretty enough. It was, after all, the depression and the time of hunger marches and the dole.

The architect chosen to design the British Pavilion was Oliver Hill, for whom Eric had worked at Morecambe. This time he asked Eric to make an exhibit typifying tennis for the sports section. Tennis was one of Eric's favourite games, and the four figures, plywood cut-outs, are convincingly poised for play in front of the background of two covered stands, each with rows of watching spectators. Behind them is a curving backcloth. On this have been painted thin linear allusions to the shapes of racquets, nettings and a garden roller. The whole scene shows perhaps something of that 'curious aloofness' that one critic had noticed about Eric's water-colours – but which he himself disliked and disclaimed.

Ravilious was also asked by the Council for Art and Industry to design the cover for the official catalogue of the British Pavilion. This was an interesting and a challenging job, and he was summoned to a meeting of a small committee under the chairmanship of A. J. Symons, and which included Herbert Read, to discuss a plan for the cover; they suggested as alternatives Britannia, a Rampant Lion, the Union Jack, and the Royal Arms – not a very inspired list, one might think. They all drank sherry at Symons' Club (the First Edition Club) and then each committee member explained the job to Ravilious according to his individual fancy. There was the usual pressure for the job to be done in a very short time.

Eric chose the Royal Arms. The drama of Edward VIII's abdication was over, and the place of the E must be taken by the G of George VI's name; his coronation would be over by the time the Paris Exhibition opened.

Eric decided to engrave his design for the cover of the catalogue. It was to be printed in two colours. It was a difficult task to combine the seriousness of a traditional symbol with a lively feeling for the present day – that is, 1937 – but it was extremely successful. He struggled hard to make it as good as possible, and in fact cut the blocks twice; the second version was simpler than the first, which had not satisfied him. Instead of the fireworks he had used on the mug, his royal beasts and the more detailed shield and crown they support were printed in blue and shown against illuminated signs, 'all glowing and sparkling with reflectors like buttons'. Eric was much relieved and very pleased to get the official letter from the Department of Overseas Trade saying that his design for the cover of the guide to the British Pavilion at the Paris Exhibition was highly commended and approved. The letter added: 'I have also yet to secure the assent of the Home Office to the use of the letters G. R.' Eric wondered, 'Could I tell them G. R. stands for Ginger Rogers?', a film star to whom he was particularly devoted.

He was next asked to design 'a gay and cheerful bouquet of rose, thistle, shamrock and leek' for the back cover. It had been decided that plans of the three floors of the British Pavilion should be printed in the catalogue, and Ravilious was asked if he could make some symbolic drawings denoting the different sections, to be used on the plans instead of words; for example, a glass bottle for the glass section – 'It may not, however, be easy to do this consistently with retaining that level of dignity which is necessary in a government publication.' How cautious they were!

After this rush of work, it was with pleasant expectations that the

The front and back cover for the catalogue for the British Pavilion at the Paris Exhibition in 1937.

Raviliouses set off on Christmas Eve to stay with Diana and Clissold Tuely, now living at Wittersham in Kent. They had not been there before and Eric was always specially keen to see new landscapes as well as to enjoy the company of his friends. They found the Tuelys living in an eighteenth-century farmhouse, built of alternating red and black brick. There was a steep hill at the back and a wide view all round of hills and frozen marshes. There were Christmas feastings and festivities, parties and expeditions. They visited the Tuelys' neighbour, Colonel Bertram Buchanan, who lived across the marsh at Iden and on whose estate Paul Nash had made the wonderful drawing of *Tench pond in a gale*, already then in the Tate. 'I took off my hat to the scene,' said Eric. The colonel owned many Nash engravings and drawings and three Samuel Palmer drawings. In Eric's opinion the best one was of a mossy barn, with two cows beautifully out of scale. (There is another version of this in the Victoria and Albert Museum.)

There was no time on this visit for Eric to do any work himself as he had to hurry back to finish off his cover for the catalogue, but he came back to Kent in the summer and did some of his best paintings there.

Chapter 9

In February 1936, Eric had had his second one-man exhibition of water-colour drawings at the Zwemmer Gallery. Thirty-eight pictures were exhibited, all priced at twelve guineas, and twenty-five were sold. The subjects of nearly all of them were landscapes in Sussex and Essex. These paintings showed a developing sureness of style, but the same fresh un-expectedness of observation expressed in a delicate formalization of the subject's elements.

Painting in watercolour was becoming more and more Eric's most important artistic activity, and when he was not working against time on other artistic jobs – also enjoyable but to a lesser degree – he was on the lookout for promising new subjects to draw.

His earliest watercolours had been rather muted in colour, even timid, but he was gradually discovering how to keep the unity of his whole colour scheme, while giving more strength to the local colour. He was conscious of this problem and worried about it. For instance, quite soon after this second show at Zwemmer's was over, he had painted a water-colour of the baker's cart from his window in Hedingham. He wrote of it: 'This picture *is* a bit too pale, and whenever I see the cart opposite in full daffodil yellow, I wish I'd laid on the colour more.' Or, a year or so later when he had been painting in Wiltshire and was working at home on two paintings begun there, he said: 'One is not bad, but I wish I could make my drawings better colour; they aren't nearly positive enough'; and of the other one; 'I've been working at the green landscape and finding the tones difficult in the foreground, but it may be moderately successful, if rather heavy in colour, gloomy enough at any rate. I so want the thing not to look washed out as they so often do.'

This was in 1937, a particularly busy year for his other activities: 'Things to be done seem to heap upon me, and fast as I do them, then more arrive. But I quite like pressure of this kind, except that I have a feeling of going round in circles like the mouse, and would rather do one thing at a time.'

One of the 'things to be done' was the complicated and laborious process of drawing out on the lithographic plates, at the Curwen Press, his illustrations for the book of shops. He had decided on his twenty-four different shops, and the designs for each were taken from notes and drawings made on the spot. The next stage was to go down to Plaistow and work on the plates at the Press.

Herbert Simon, one of the directors at that time, remembers Eric 'delighting in an easy contact with the skilled men who actually did the lithographic plate preparation and printing. He liked the 'works' atmos-phere, and as he had no feelings of being a superior person, he was offered friendship from all unreservedly.'

Each illustration was to be printed in four different colours, with a

The Causeway, Wiltshire Downs April 1937. Watercolour. 17½″ × 21½″. Signed. This was first exhibited at the Memorial Exhibition in 1948.
Victoria & Albert Museum

lithographic plate for each colour; Eric had to work out the colour separation and draw what was needed on each plate, and of course to choose the colours he wanted. One combination of four colours was used for eight illustrations, another set of four colours was used for another eight, and a third mixture for the remaining eight.

Eric used his medium so inventively, varying the proportions of the four colours on each plate, and altering their hue and tone by superimposing one on the other, that most people looking through the book would probably not realize that the number of actual colour printings was so limited.

Eric's friend, J. M. Richards, who had shared in the discovery of some of the shops, was commissioned to write the short text, aimed to interest children as well as their elders. It was exactly right: a factual account of each kind of shop, with fascinating information learnt from the actual shops about what they sold. For instance, in the Model Ships and Railways shop, Bassett Lowke, there were model railway stations, as well as every kind of locomotive, rolling stock and track. Three stations could be completely equipped with everything you would expect to find there, including model railwaymen and model passengers. In the cheaper sets of figures to stand on the platform the passengers were ordinary people, but in the most expensive sets, they consisted of George Bernard Shaw, Charlie Chaplin, Lloyd George, Stanley Baldwin, Amy Johnson and Ramsay MacDonald.

Among the other kinds of shops chosen by Eric were those of a Fire Engineer, Theatrical Properties, Cheesemonger, Clerical Outfitter's, Oyster Bar and Submarine Engineer; this last was one that Eric and Edward Bawden had first noticed on their way to and from Morley College, when they were painting the murals for the refreshment room there in 1930.

Perhaps one of the most successful is Mr Pollard's, 'Naturalist: Furrier:

Baker's Cart
*Watercolour. 18" ×
22½". This is one of a
number of Castle
Hedingham subjects
exhibited at Zwemmer's
in 1936.
Mrs Guy Hepher*

Plumassier', as he inscribed himself over his shop window, which displayed tiger and leopard skins, a bear's head and an animal skull with huge twisting horns. The actual shop was near Baker Street, but was destroyed in the war. The title chosen for the book was *High Street*, suggested by Charlotte Bawden's friend Gwyneth Lloyd-Thomas.

Though doing all this work at the Curwen Press took up time which might have been spent painting, the experiments with colour lithography must have added to Eric's discoveries about using transparent colours in his watercolours, just as the skills he had developed when working with these paints had enabled him to produce a successful lithograph at his first attempt. One skill enriched the other, and each generated its own excitement. This two-way relationship, but in the management of tone rather than colour, can also be noted in his wood engravings. In textures and patterning, the influence of engraving is very noticeable in the brushwork of his watercolours.

He had been working lately on two books to be illustrated with wood engravings. One was the *Country Life Cookery Book*, written by Ambrose Heath, and decorated by Ravilious with engraved chapter headings, each designed in an oval. The general plan for these was an enlarged still-life in the foreground of a landscape: for example, fishes, a fish basket and a lobster, in front of a distant channel steamer coming into Newhaven docks, or some round melons with a net-like outer skin seen large against a corner of the Brick House garden. The engravings have beautifully balanced tones, light areas predominating. This cookery book was published in 1937.

The other book was one he worked on with special enthusiasm. A few years earlier, in 1930, an exciting new breakthrough in publishing had

High Street, written by J. M. Richards, illustrated by Eric Ravilious (Country Life, 1938). **Above** *Naturalist: Furrier: Plumassier – Mr Pollard once stuffed a pair of elephants for the Marquess of Bute!* **Below** *Fireworks – 'an ordinary newspaper shop and tobacconist's, but for a few weeks before November 5th every year it fills its windows with fireworks.'*

been launched by Allen Lane: this was Penguin Books, providing paperbacks to sell for sixpence each. They were a great success and there was soon a scheme to produce a series of Illustrated Classics, with Robert Gibbings as the art editor; he asked Ravilious if he would like to design one. Eric felt he had had enough of Illustrated Classics in the past and turned down this offer, but another from the Nonesuch Press was more tempting and was for a book he particularly loved. Here is the letter he received from the Nonesuch production manager in May 1937:

Dear Ravilious,

We want to do a limited edition of White's Selborne. Do you feel inclined to do some wood engravings for it? I think, myself, that the subjects should be rural scenery rather than careful pictures of the birds and flowers that White mentions by name. I fancy that 24 small wood-cuts is about the best number. If you would like and would be able to do it before next September, I would ask you to let me know your fee and to do one or two specimen blocks.

Yours sincerely,
Harry Carter

Eric replied that he would like to make engravings for this new edition of the *History of Selborne*. The first thing to do was to visit Selborne. He and Tirzah drove there and stayed for a few days; the place still seemed very much as Gilbert White had described it, and they could explore the paths and woods behind the wakes, as well as the church and village.

The book was to be produced in two volumes, with an introduction and text selected and edited by H. J. Massingham. The first volume was to include the *Natural History* and the *Naturalist's Journal*, and the second the *Antiquities, Poems* and *Correspondence*.

Eric started on the job with great enthusiasm and produced title pages for each volume that perfectly express the spirit of Gilbert White's writings and have a convincing eighteenth-century flavour. In Volume I, the artist has shown Gilbert White and his friend Thomas Pennant discussing a book about birds; for Volume II he chose the interior of Selborne Church, with a view of the churchyard seen through the open door.

Engraving from the Nonesuch Press edition of **The Natural History of Selborne** *by Gilbert White, 1938.*

The other illustrations, headpieces for each chapter, are very attractive as decorations, and very accomplished as engravings; but some of them seem to show less feeling for Gilbert White's own attitude and descriptions than the title pages. For instance, in the engraving of Gilbert White examining the dead female moose hung up in a greenhouse, one would never guess from his calm and detached attitude that its stench was overpowering. And, unlike the male, the female moose does not have those massive antlers that Ravilious has depicted. David Garnett pointed this out in his review of the book when it first came out.

However, the publishers and editor were delighted and Harry Carter wrote on 19 April 1938: 'At last I can send you a Selborne, and do so with my best congratulations. The printing is poor in places but I do not think you ever appeared to better advantage.'

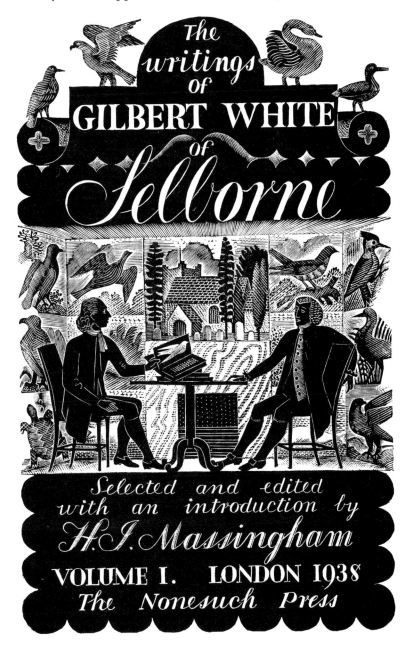

*The title page to Volume I of Gilbert White's **The Natural History of Selborne** (The Nonesuch Press, 1938).*

In the autumn of 1938, Richard Smart, of Arthur Tooth and Sons Ltd, had been discussing with Eric the possibility of his having his next show of paintings at their gallery in New Bond Street. It was decided that it should be held in their Front Gallery from 11 May to 3 June in the next year. Eric's first consideration was the need to collect enough paintings good enough in his own estimation for this exhibition.

He had already had a concentrated month and a half of painting in Breconshire that spring, staying at a farm at Capel-y-Ffin, near Llanthony. It was early February and he wrote:

> It is rather boisterous weather but improving a little. The skies are superb but the hills so massive it is difficult to leave room for them on the paper. Mrs Saunders and all her family are as nice as possible and they are all so good-looking and so large on the female side – she cooks in the most generous way and I don't know how to eat these great platefuls of pig's fry. A pig has been hanging up in the kitchen and to-day was scientifically cut up like a diagram in a cookery book, and I watched it simply fascinated. You should have seen them burning off the bristles with flaming bracken, with the pig on a stretcher. It was like a funeral pyre and the smell was amazing.

For most of the time he saw no one but Mrs Saunders and her family, so it was an excitement and a delight to be visited by another artist, John Piper, who had also been working in Wales. He and his wife, Myfanwy, took Eric down to the pub for a meal and they all drank beer and talked. They then went back to the farm and looked at John's paper pictures – collages of Welsh chapels, lovely gay colours, and some very good beach scenes. Piper said he might do as many as three a day, an ability that Eric frankly envied. He himself had been having trouble controlling his water-colour washes outdoors, the weather lately having been so bitingly cold and the wind so fierce. He found that too much working indoors from memory gave bad results, and it was not until early March that it suddenly became warm and sunny. 'I work simply all day,' he wrote:

> trying to make up for lost time and bad drawings, with much better results. A painting of a water-wheel [home-made by the son of the farmer, out of chunks of wood and the bottoms of petrol tins] is now almost finished and looks rather well, and a bit Chinese; also there are four geese in the picture, and the time is eight in the morning.

While Eric was painting in Wales, Tirzah had been busy making her marbled papers. She sold some to the Victoria and Albert Museum, to the Little Gallery, and to Dunbar Hay. There is an ecstatic letter from A. J. Symons about some she had made for him. She also invited her parents for a short visit and they came to stay on 2 March. Colonel Garwood's diary for 1938 notes: 'T. met us in her car at Chelmsford . . . she made a great effort to entertain us and we slept in her bedroom. She was with John in the nursery. Both her little maids sleep out . . . T. had a tea-party for us . . . she seems very popular and knows everybody in the village. . .' 4 March: 'Tirzah and Ella [Mrs Garwood] went to a tea-party, leaving me to look after John. I put on his zip-fronted pants three times wrong. He is very quick to get into mischief and emptied Tirzah's marbling paints into a tub of water.' There were more visits to neighbours and 'Tirzah showed us the wood-cuts for the forthcoming edition of Gilbert White's *Selborne*, and also some of Eric's mugs.'

New Year Snow 1935.
Watercolour. 18" × 22".
Painted at Capel-y-Ffin,
Breconshire, this was
exhibited in 1939 at
Arthur Tooth & Sons.
Private Collection

One of the things that Eric had asked Tirzah to do for him while he was in the wilds of Wales was to arrange the first showing of his crockery at the Wedgwood Trade Display in Hatton Garden. He had been told there would be a table reserved for his designs.

Once back at home from Llanthony, there was plenty of work waiting for Eric. The Department of Overseas Trade, for instance, was wanting a map of the British Commonwealth, as well as another catalogue cover design, this time for the United Kingdom Government Pavilion at the 1939 New York World's Fair. 'The New York Fair', he wrote to his mother-in-law, 'still keeps me busy. The map is enormously big, and my Britannia for the catalogue has been turned down at once. Her figure was too matronly they said, so now it is another Royal Arms.' Looking now at the engraving it is hard to understand the objection to Britannia's outline – a concession to American taste perhaps. There was also to be an exhibition of modern British painting in connection with the World's Fair, and the Tate Gallery had asked to borrow three of Eric's water-colours for it. And there was work for Wedgwood to be done from time to time: a Christmas dinner service was produced in July.

But he managed to fit in more painting visits, such as a week at Aldeburgh, painting bathing machines and a life-boat. The painter Vivian Pitchforth, a Royal College contemporary, was staying at Tollesbury Creek that summer and has written: 'I was living on a boat, and went on deck, bleary-eyed, to look at what God Almighty had to offer early in the morning, and there was Rav already at it.' Eric had been there for a week drawing yachts; one 'was the most elegant thing I've seen for some time and a sort of plum colour and white, with varnish yellow masts.'

When describing this meeting, what Eric remembered was being introduced to Pitch's companion as, 'This is Ravilious who sells all his pictures; he and Bawden are a proper couple of Ethel M. Dells – only better aesthetically.'

Before this, Eric had also been to the Tuelys at Wittersham to paint the country he had liked so much at Christmas. He drew greenhouses in Kent – a beautiful painting of an interior with geraniums and carnations – after unsuccessful attempts to draw the unfamiliar landscapes of Romney Marsh. He went on to Rye Harbour to paint, staying at the William the Conqueror Inn. The artist Edward Le Bas, who was staying at his cottage nearby, saw the landscape Eric was painting and liked it so much he bought it on the spot (it was lent for the next show, of course). The next place to be visited was Dungeness and this was also fruitful.

The last painting visit that year was to Bristol with John Nash. He and Eric had got to know each other at the Royal College, where they were both on the staff; Eric's first visit to John and Christine's home at Meadle in Buckinghamshire was in the winter of 1937 when the wooded hills all round were covered with snow. He had enjoyed it enormously. The two artists went out to try and draw, but the snow wet the paper so much it was no use going on. Nash paid a return visit to Hedingham the next year and enjoyed drawing the sand-pits where Eric himself had had several failures the year before.

Some years earlier, in the 1920s, John Nash had been much inspired by painting in Bristol, and he told Eric it was the best port in England, so they planned together a painting visit there. They went in November, and John Nash found they could still take the rooms in Cornwallis Crescent, above the Hotwells Road and the Avon, where he had stayed before. He remembers now how excited Eric was by what he was seeing for the first time, his own reactions being inevitably more staid. They were both keen to work by night, when the pleasure steamers – laid up in their winter quarters – looked beautifully ghostly by artificial light. This sometimes meant drawing by day and painting from memory at home, and John was impressed by the way Eric settled down to work in the crowded little sitting-room; he used to try out the colours he was mixing on a separate sheet of paper, before using them on his painting.

One evening, however, when Eric had decided to go on drawing outside after dark, and was working intently on his picture of a paddle steamer, he had suddenly heard a grinding noise and a voice calling out, 'lucky for you I saw you, old cock, or you'd have been a box of cold meat.' Eric had set up his easel, without noticing it was on the tracks of one of those light railways that are used in the docks.

The show at Tooth's was to open in May; there was a little time left. While on a family visit to Eastbourne he wrote to Diana Tuely:

We explored Beachy Head in the sun this morning, and Belle Toute (the lighthouse) and the Cuckmere, and as there is not much hope of my getting away to France just yet, I shall draw there all the time I can. It is a good sight in the sun and a considerable variety of scene – an immense bar of light on the sea is splendid and must be done. I began work there on a projecting bit of cliff about four yards square, but flat and comfortable, and looked into the eye of the sun as long as it could be borne – the sun is no trouble, it is the wind I don't like. Tirzah is taking me up again after supper to see how the light looks.

Beachy Head
Watercolour. 17" × 23".
Exhibited at Arthur
Tooth's in 1939, this
shows the Belle Toute
lighthouse.
Private Collection

It might be possible to paint – something like this –

Eric managed to get over to France in March for some more harbour scenes; he went to Normandy, staying at St Valery-en-Caux and Le Havre. He found comfortable quarters on the quay in a room three flights up, and drew on the quay till he could stand the cold no longer, and then painted indoors. He enjoyed meal times in the café below, watching 'the powerful and voluble dockers, rivetters and fitters who filled it. They wear such nice clothes, blue trousers and berets, and throw bread about and laugh out loud. They are far larger than most Frenchmen; looking around it is hard to imagine the French losing a war.'

He got back from Le Havre in April and took these last paintings straight to Tooth's Gallery.

He had been exchanging information about promising places to paint and to stay in with Edward Wadsworth, a painter of a slightly older generation and also a lover of harbour scenes, who had lately been painting at Newhaven. Here is his letter to Eric:

Dairy House, Maresfield Park, Sussex
17.5.39

Dear Ravilious,

Many thanks for your letter and the information about Dungeness. If I decide to go there I shall write to the postman (H. M. Postman) and ask him to put his mother in touch with me – mentioning your name, if I may.

Also thanks a lot for your description of Fécamp which, as I said, I have only driven through – you make it sound even better than I had imagined – St Valerie I don't know, but Le Havre I have know intimately for over 30 years and was indeed there last summer for a little time. It is a real gold mine of matter. Of course I knew the buoy yard you mention and have done various drawings of those objects. I feel, though, that I personally must beware of ready-made geometry.

Shall you be at the meeting at 32 St James Street – 5.30 on Tuesday next? If so we might have a quick drink afterwards.

> Many thanks again,
> Yours,
> Edward Wadsworth

The show opened on 11 May and went on until 3 June. Ravilious shared the gallery with another artist, Timothy Eden, but they each had a room of their own. Eric's friends were naturally pleased to hear that the Tooth's man at the door had said to Eric, 'We can tell which are your people, they look more intelligent.'

The show was a great success. There was no doubt that Eric's work had developed and matured remarkably in the three years since his last show. He himself felt this and that for the first time his paintings were no longer tentative but expressed what he had been aiming at and had been searching for, for so long.

The critics recognized this. Eric Newton, for instance, wrote in the *Observer*:

> The quality of Mr. Ravilious' watercolours at Tooth's Galleries seems to me almost untranslatable. All the qualities dear to watercolourists – a full flowing brush, a facile exploitation of the charm of the medium – are nothing to him. He paints as a child paints, obsessed with his meaning. The fact that he is a fine craftsman and an eloquent draughts-man is secondary. I had never realized the wiriness of wire netting before looking at his *Cliffs in March*. With few exceptions each of his watercolours contains a new revelation of this kind. In *Salt Marsh* it is the helplessness of a derelict boat, in *Beachy Head* the piercing beam of a lighthouse, in *Room at the William the Conqueror* a set of lace-curtains and a patterned wall-paper, in *Cuckmere Valley* a meandering river, in *Wiltshire Landscape* a rolling road.

And Jan Gordon wrote in *The Sunday Times*:

> Between the acts of seeing and of perceiving a gulf lies. Of talented artists the majority do but see, clearly perhaps, hypnotically sometimes, but moments of extra-perception are rare. Of these watercolours by Ravilious one may feel that a large number of them do touch true perception. No matter what the subject may be, a sandpit, a country lane in a drizzle, a broken water-turbine lying in a stream, the window of a pub-room with a spangled ceiling, a farmhouse bedroom, an old boat on the mud, or Beachy Head and its lighthouse, each by a com-bination of unexpected selection, exactly apt colour, and an almost prestidigitous watercolour technique and textural variety, appear as something magic, almost mystic, distilled out of the ordinary everyday.

Eric was elated by the success of the show and wrote in answer to a letter congratulating him: 'Last Sunday's *Observer* had the best notice, unless the next *Sunday Times* beats it. I feel set up and a bit above myself, like Balbus, whose head was crowned with a garland. This is a kind of reward for the lumbago and the March winds on Beachy Head.'

Buoyed up, perhaps, by the impact of seeing his last three years' paintings collected together, Eric went on to do a series of watercolours of some of the chalk figures cut in the Downs of Southern England. He

The Vale of the White Horse c1939. Watercolour. 17³/₄" × 21³/₄". Signed. Trustees of The Tate Gallery, London

had always loved the Long Man of Wilmington, cut in the Sussex Downs not far from Eastbourne, and he started by making a painting of him. He felt it was 'quite a good one, I do believe', one of his best in fact. (It was bought soon after by the Victoria and Albert Museum.) He then went to Weymouth to paint King George III riding his horse on a hill above the town, to Cerne Abbas for the splendid giant, to Westbury for an eighteenth-century horse and to Uffington for the much earlier white horse on its hill. The striking thing about these four paintings is their ingenious variety. Each happens to be a record of a chalk figure, but each seems to be seen in a different way, and each gives one a shock of surprise; most of all the Westbury Horse seen from a railway carriage. He drew it from the train, going back and forth between two stations and painting from the interior of the third-clas carriage. Seen out of the top of the left-hand window, the standing white horse shows small but unmistakable.

By the summer of 1939 it was difficult to think about anything but the perpetual state of crisis in Europe, and Hitler's ever-increasing threat to peace. In the last few years many artists and poets and other creative workers, who might not have been interested in ordinary party politics, had realized that liberty of thought and artistic expression were in danger and had joined with left-wing sympathizers in protests of different kinds. In 1937, for instance, artists sent work to a great international exhibition, 'Artists against Fascism', in a house in Grosvenor Square. Eric had sent a picture called 'Sport', and the next year one of his watercolour landscapes. He also allowed his name to appear on a list of artists willing to undertake a commission for a patron, who then paid half the money to the cause. He had been asked to do a painting for Lord Faringdon of

Chalk Figure near
Weymouth c1939.
Watercolour. 17½" ×
21¾".
The National Gallery of
Canada, Ottawa

Buscot Park, which he found a congenial task.

The news was getting worse every day. The war that had been threatening so long now seemed inevitable. Eric felt acutely unsettled. He had always hated uncertainty and could not bear the feeling of drifting along or even of just waiting. As a way of ending this he even thought of enlisting in the Artists' Rifles, and wrote to John Nash, who as a very young man had fought in the trenches in France with that regiment in the First World War until he and his brother Paul were appointed official war artists in 1917. John begged him not to do anything rash, he did not think he would find many artists there, and 'peace-time soldiering must be deadly and after all it is still what is known as peacetime . . . don't rush in.' Geoffrey Fry, who had also been in the First World War, was asked for advice. He replied: 'I still think it would be ridiculous waste for you to be an ordinary infantryman or doing anything but where you would be more use than the ordinary chap' – this was on the 24 July 1939.

Uncertainty ended on 1 September with Neville Chamberlain telling the country on the wireless that we were now at war with Germany.

Observer posts, to monitor all aeroplanes flying over England, were immediately set up on all the hills of England, by the Royal Observer Corps. As soon as possible Eric took on a part-time job at the Hedingham Post. John Nash did the same at his local post in Buckinghamshire.

Eric and his artist friends' experiences in wartime can be most vividly described by themselves. Letter-writing took on a new importance, as they found themselves in strange places and new situations and told each other about them. Eric had always enjoyed writing letters, particularly about his work, and he wrote a great many. So these final chapters can be largely told in Eric's own words.

Chapter 10

September 10th

My dear Helen,

Here is a picture of me saving the country. I work at odd hours of the day and night watching aeroplanes up on the hill, and work with a partner – not in the picture – we wear life-boatmen's outfits against the weather and tin hats for show. It is like a Boys' Own Paper story, what with spies and passwords and all manner of nonsense: all the same as far as wars go, it is a congenial job, and the scene lovely, mushrooms about and blackberries coming along and the most spectacular sunrises.

Where, Helen, are you in all this? Write and tell me what you are doing.

All work seems to have come to an end, although I can't be sure of that yet, and there isn't much impulse to work either; in fact, it was a relief to get something more or less useful to do (at 15/- a week) in this Observer Corps.

Tirzah comes back tomorrow from Eastbourne with John and James, the new baby. I am rather well looked after by an aged granny from Wood Green who is billetted here with three grand-children, all boys. She makes wonderful sandwiches to take up at nights to the post. It will be a full house.

Some day I must show you the one good picture painted this summer of the Wilmington Giant.

Love from Eric

General post was the order of the day. Eric had wanted to have a talk with Edward Bawden, whose letter below explains why it had not yet been possible.

Brick House, Gt Bardfield, Essex
Sept. 9, 1939

Dear Eric,

I am sorry I missed seeing you last Friday when you called but I was still in Zurich and remained there until the afternoon of the same day. The Swiss Exhibition closed down upon us while we were in the grounds having lunch and it was then that we heard of fighting having commenced on the Polish frontier. I have been meaning to write and congratulate you and Tirzah on having a second boy. You are lucky in having a run on the male sex. If you are writing to Tirzah give her my love. I hope she is taking things peacefully at Castle Garwood. The young fellow is probably screaming his head off at having appeared at such an inopportune moment of unsettled international relationships.

What part do you intend to play in the general mess? I wonder if the following addresses are of any use to you: the first two refer to camouflage, the last for propaganda: [addresses for the Air Ministry, the O.C.R.E. and the Ministry of Labour followed.]

Yours
Edward

More from Eric about the observer post in a letter to Diana Tuely:

It is a full moon again tonight so my 8–midnight watch will be a pleasant one. I've taken to doing a little drawing up there at quiet times, hoping I won't get caught, but conditions are too difficult to do much. We get Germans over from time to time and then of course it is a buzz of activity and excitement. Did you see anything of the Kent raid the other day? I wondered if Clissold's gun had been in action again. My name is down for one or two things and perhaps some more definite job will come along next year. They may be giving me a permit to draw guns and military things soon, but there is so little chance to do much here. Dungeness would be the place now, and if I ever do give up observing, I shall find another Dungeness. . . .

The soldiers here gave an oyster party (the first oysters since Whitstable) and we had two dozen apiece with brown ale and bread and butter. Tirzah ordered and ate a whole lobster.

And the following day we asked the whole searchlight party in to eat large hares, which they did with ease, and played progressive ping-pong after, round our table. The noise of military boots was like thunder.

A barrage balloon has broken loose again and trailed its rope over the country fusing lights for miles round.

It is a nuisance working with candles. Time goes along in a special way. I mean one doesn't notice it as a person waiting for a train might, and I think it is not long or short but a vacuum, and ideas and feelings eddy a little but don't flow.

It was good to hear you say that work is in the air again because I am beginning to feel that way too and it is nice to find someone else panting to paint.

A month later Eric was writing to Cecilia Dunbar Kilburn. She was now running the Dunbar Hay shop by herself, Athole Hay having had a sudden illness and died, tragically young, in 1938.

> Bank House, Castle Hedingham, Essex
> Nov. 16th

Dear Cecilia,

Thank you for your instructions for playing carpet bowls – we mean to try out our half dozen this evening. Did I ever tell you about 'Boule', if that is the way to spell it? The French bowling game, with heavy metal balls, where you can play on any surface and use the natural hazards, trees and gravel paths and concrete. It really is a marvellous game, and if you could get the sets of balls over from France, or better, have the set made here, I'm sure anyone would buy them. I played just before the war in Chermayeff's garden on a fine Sunday evening. [Serge Chermayeff, partner of Eric Mendelsohn, who built the De la Warr Pavilion on the front at Eastbourne in 1933–36].

Observing still goes on here and I do very little work. The Underground have accepted my poster. You remember I came up partly to see ice-skating: and there seems to be a feeling of work in the air, even the possibility of a book. Nothing of course definite, least of all from the War Office. Official artists won't be seen at work this year I'm sure, and probably not till the spring. The thing is that they have a fair-sized list to choose from and I feel no certainty of being in the first batch: though I think that anyway they will give me permission to draw. I do very much look forward to this, and long to make a beginning. . . .

By the way, Wedgwood's have sent at last completed samples of the Christmas pudding set, and have made a very good job of it . . . but not for this Christmas, alas.

> Tirzah sends her love,
> Yours,
> Eric

The book he referred to was the one of the Chalk Figures.

At last, on Christmas Eve, this letter came from the Admiralty:

Dear Ravilious,

You may have heard rumours of a scheme which is now being launched for having various phases of the war recorded by selected artists working for the Government. The Admiralty has already appointed one official whole-time artist, and you and John Nash have been selected to work for the Admiralty on a part-time basis, if you should be willing. We very much hope that the idea will appeal to you; indeed it would be a great disappointment to the Admiralty, the Ministry of Information, and, I may add, myself, if you should feel unable or unwilling to undertake work of this kind.

If you should be willing, please let me know here as soon as you can and tell me when you could come and see me to discuss details. From our point of view, the sooner you get to work the better. Perhaps I should say that the Treasury have already approved the necessary expenditure.

Yours sincerely
R. Gleadowe

Eric was wildly excited and accepted at once. With his usual punctuality he longed to start immediately, and was already promising Tirzah to bring her back 'parrots and monkeys and all those kinds of things'. There were to be interviews with E. M. O'R. Dickey at the Ministry of Information as well as with Gleadowe at the Admiralty. It was essential for them to be in uniform as they would be working in prohibited areas, and, 'They say that a captain of the Royal Marines is less conspicuous on land (it is a khaki uniform) and without responsibilities or embarrassments at sea, so that is what they are going to make us.' Eric and John Nash compared notes, as this letter shows:

Meadle
Saturday night

My dear Eric,

I was at the M. of I. on Friday playing truant part of the time from College and heard from Dickey that you had been there. I don't suppose I have anything more to report than you have – they talk of sending us a 'contract letter' but that only deals with the finance and I have heard nothing from the Admiralty since I went there. When I was there I broached the subject of commissioned rank to Gleadowe and there seemed no difficulties. Captainships seemed as cheap as farthing buns and it seemed as if one only missed being made a Major because one had to recognize Muirhead Bone's seniority! But I begin to doubt now if Gleadowe really has the authority to promise these insignia – we must continue to wait and see I suppose. . . .

I went to College yesterday and saw most of 'the boys'. Form was good or even above average and Percy [Horton] made a fine story of a week spent teaching the *Punch* artist H. M. Bateman to paint. Dickey tells me that the Army War Artists are to be dressed in War Correspondents' uniform with W.C. on the hat band – rather shaming – so I'm glad you and I are in the Senior Service!

Let me know if you hear anything fresh.

Yours ever,
John

Warship in Dock
Commissioned 1940. LD
70. Watercolour. 17" ×
22". Probably Chatham.
Imperial War Museum,
London

Three of the artists officially appointed to be war correspondents with the army were Barnett Freedman, Edward Ardizzone and Edward Bawden.

Edward wrote in a Christmas letter to Tirzah, 'Tell Eric that I accepted the camouflage appointment but have since chucked it, thereby casting my bread, – nearly dry bread now – upon troubled waters – with a gesture of wild abandon. This sort of feckless behaviour on the part of one so prudent as myself cannot but move him to admiration.'

At last, after frustrating delays, which made him feel 'like Lot's wife, caught on one leg, half turned to salt' – Eric found himself in early February at the Royal Naval Barracks, Chatham, and wrote this letter from there to me:

I wanted to write to you, but have been busy about so many unfamiliar things I've not done any writing to speak of. Work is biting cold when there is a wind, but two drawings – snow of course – are on the way. It is lovely doing some drawing again: and this uniform keeps most people off even in crowded docks and places, though I am looked on with the utmost suspicion and produce my sheaf of passes at intervals all day. The Mess is a wonderful place, huge and tasteless, but very nice food, and even nicer drinks. Then you go off into an equally big lounge and drink port, captains and commanders, admirals and lieutenants all about in two's and three's, and very pink and jocular and 'damn it sir' – I do like them, and they are very indulgent about my many breaches of etiquette and extraordinarily kind and helpful – I hardly dare mention any simple idea I may have in case they set going some elaborate machinery to bring it about. You would be impressed by the Navy I think – they are so handsome, clean, pink, immaculate and set such standards for one who is in khaki and not any of these things – I scrub away at my hands and brush my hair, but it is no good, lacking

115

Ship's Screw on Truck
Commissioned 1940. LD
66. Watercolour. 16¾" ×
22¼".
Ashmolean Museum,
Oxford.

the fundamentals. One of them told me tonight about 'Red Biddy' – you ask for a small port in a large glass and fill it up with methylated spirit. It sounds awful. He says you can set light to the urine after.

Tomorrow I've an etiquette course and a gas course. The saluting is appalling in a barracks and when in addition you meet a platoon of 30 or 40 men and the sergeant gives the 'Eyes Right', it is hard not to laugh. They do this with an unbelievable efficiency, and a fixed look – The sentries plunge bayonets at you after dark, and you have to be quick remembering who you are. . . . The figureheads about the place are lovely – I long to draw them . . . I'd like to show you my drawings – now I must go to bed in my cabin in the roof.

One of his first paintings was of a *Ship's Screw on a Railway Truck*, in a snowscape (the newspapers had just been allowed to mention that England had had the severest spell of frost since 1894), but Eric felt there was not enough to be seen of war activities in these surroundings of factories and foundries, and decided to move on to Sheerness, of which several of the naval officers he had met spoke well.

From the Royal Fountain Hotel, Sheerness, he wrote:

I have just reached here from an exhilarating weekend with a naval party at Whitstable. After Chatham, it was like being let out of school, and I managed a drawing, or very nearly, and was out in a small boat for hours in what seemed to me a rough sea. This was the best sort of outing, packed with excitement, and it is a pity I can't tell you about it – May it happen again.

Dangerous Work at Low Tide
Commissioned 1940. LD 71. Watercolour. 28½" × 31½". Painted on the coast near Whitstable in early 1940.
The Admiralty, London

The object of this mini-expedition was to salve a German magnetic mine, only the second one to be washed up on the English shores. For this exploit, the two naval officers, Commander Obbard and Lieutenant West, were each awarded the D.S.C., which pleased Eric very much when he read about it in the paper some time afterwards. The drawing he did of it was shown at the first War Artists' Exhibition, under the title of *Rendering Mines Safe*. For some reason this was later officially changed to *Dangerous Work at Low Tide*.

Sheerness, itself, that is to say the docks – is good – and lovely Regency buildings, almost Venetian in parts, and oh, the still-life of buoys, anchors, chains and wreckage! I must try to remember what *I* am here for, and only do one drawing of this kind. . . . This pub is full of bored air force men drinking and talking shop – small departmental war talk is simply maddening going on as it does all day.

His next port of call was Grimsby – 'rather a dull featureless town' he called it in a letter to Cecilia Dunbar Kilburn written on 24 April. It went on:

The docks are nice and I work there all day but won't be sorry either to go to sea from here or get away somewhere and finish the drawings – of divers, destroyers, oropesa floats, lightships and guns. Drawing is difficult because of the wind in this flat exposed place, high winds and a smell of fish: however, today was the first really calm one and perhaps the fine spell has begun.

There are trains all night outside my bedroom window and an insis-

Barrage Balloons outside a British Port
Commissioned 1940. LD 68. Watercolour. 17$\frac{1}{3}$" × 21". Probably Sheerness, Isle of Sheppey.
Leeds City Art Galleries

tent whistling which now I am used to and sleep through the noise, but find I have odd dreams – on Monday, that I was aboard a paddle steamer gliding with speed and perfect smoothness round hairpin bends of a river. There was a gibbous moon and a sun with six rays, like this, in the sky together, and a coppery sultry atmosphere. Then I was aboard another, and this time it was stationary and it was of some particular significance, and I had to go there. And last night, I dreamed that I was one of those small country buses and there was someone making a long arm as it were and steering from a back seat. It was very heavy going, and an erratic course dodging parcels of shopping like Christmas presents scattered over the road. I put all this down to the trains by night.

How are you? I hope well and flourishing. Do you know Wedgwood's are actually producing the third and last mug? It is a commemorative piece of J.W. and lithographed – Tirzah is sending it for me to see this week. . . .

I believe you could sell Oropesa Floats in your shop.

> Yours ever,
> Eric

In a letter to Tirzah from Grimsby he wrote:

Today I have been at work on the Bridge of a Destroyer which is a mass of speaking tubes like some sort of sprouting African lily. Next week, I hope to have a shot at the Engine room which is intestinal and infernal. I messed up a beautiful beginning on the Bridge of my escort vessel but I shall try again as a lithograph. . . .

Thank you too for the *Statesman* – it was like a breath of fresh Bloomsbury air in this place and this hotel. One is surprised to find all

Midnight Sun
*Commissioned 1940. LD
280. Watercolour. 17¾"
× 22½". Signed and
dated June 1940.
Trustees of the Tate
Gallery, London*

these interests still going on . . . I am working hard, but not very well really, yet, though one drawing may be a good one.

When at Grimsby Eric had been offered a week at sea on a destroyer escorting trawlers, which he was pleased about, but at the last moment this was put off, as all sailing orders were altered. So he decided to finish off all the paintings he had begun in the quiet of his home, until his next assignment, which was to be much the most adventurous one yet. I heard from him in the middle of May. 'I am going off to Norway this week, with the lieutenant I know, (who lives in Hedingham). . . .

This is a letter he wrote from the ship:

My dear H.B.

We are in port again – but a very remote port – for an hour or so and then back where we came from, at least that coast.

We have been in the Arctic as high as 70° 30′, which I looked up and was delighted to see how far north it was. So I've done drawings of the midnight sun and the hills of the Chankly Bore – I simply loved it, especially the sun. It was so nice working on deck long past midnight in bright sunshine – it never fell below the horizon and at its lowest was about 2″ (reduced to paper scale) from sea level.

I do like the life and the people, in fact it is about the first time since the war I've felt any peace of mind or desire to work. It is so remote and lovely in these parts and the excitements, from above and below, don't interrupt much. If they were to allow women aboard all would be perfect – I mentioned this in the war room but they all said no and that it was a bad idea and would make a lot of trouble. They should take the risk.

He was away at sea for a month: 'the excitements from above and

Norway 1940
Commissioned 1940. LD
68. Watercolour. 17¾" ×
22".
Laing Art Gallery, Tyne
and Wear County
Museums Service.

below' were of course attacks by German aeroplanes, mines or submarines. The Norwegian battles, on sea and on land, had begun in early April. 'We have had a few excitements, at which I have leaped (allowing for the roll) to the deck, pencil in hand.' The sailors were astonished at his concentration on drawing during these attacks.

He wrote to Diana Tuely:

H.M.S. Highlander

It has been a wonderful trip with excitements here and there from planes and submarines, but the grand thing was going up into the Arctic Circle with a brilliant sun shining all night, Arctic terns flying by the ship – I simply loved it and in fact haven't enjoyed anything so much since the war. The sun is much hotter there than you think and I work without a coat quite comfortably. At sea people wear all sorts of clothes . . . and the whole time we have to wear a rubber life-belt, even in bed, and keep it partly blown up, so that everyone presents a chest like a guardsman. . . .

Now having at last got into harbour out of the fog we are to sail first thing in the morning. There will be some excitement this time I think. . . . It is strange not seeing land, or women or darkness for so long. It is like some unearthly existence.

Eric had brought back pictures to which he gave titles like *Norway 1940*, *H.M.S. Glorious in the Arctic*, *Midnight Sun*, *Leaving Scapa Flow* and two of *Ark Royal in Action*. He worked intensively at finishing them and others in time for the first exhibition of war artists' paintings held at the National Gallery at the beginning of July. (The Permanent Collection had of course been moved to safety at the beginning of the war.) He was told they had given satisfaction to the War Artists' Committee and several people, including Francis Meynell, wrote to tell him how much they admired them.

Photographs of them were sent to him at his next base. This was Portsmouth, and here are some of his descriptions for Tirzah of his life there:

23 July – I am torn between interiors and landscapes – I mean seascapes – and make rather a mess of both. Interiors are not easy. You must get them dark enough, and I feel that I've drawn enough sea. . . . I'm trying too many sorts of things probably – The air-raids are no help as we have to run for it to shelter and that is a great bore at nights as lights all go out in three minutes. . . . Today as the siren blew I ran into Augustine Courtauld [The Arctic explorer and a war-time lieutenant R.N.V.R. He was a neighbour of Eric and Tirzah at Great Yeldham] and shall be dining in his mess this evening.

They are taking me out in an M.T.B. tomorrow. They go like the wind and wet you to the skin. God send I'm not sick as well.

The Admiral – the C. in C. – is very like Millais to look at; a naval Millais, and is a nephew in fact. He is very helpful. You know he *is* Bubbles, and called by that name by the Navy. At a grand lunch today,

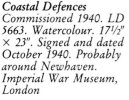

Coastal Defences
Commissioned 1940. LD 5663. Watercolour. 17½" × 23". Signed and dated October 1940. Probably around Newhaven. Imperial War Museum, London

he was in cracking form all the time. You would dote on him – he is like a figurehead, and would make a fine one. [Tirzah was coming for the next weekend.] I still draw submarine interiors exclusively and hope to have something to show you when you come.

His next address was H.M.S. *Dolphin*, Gosport, Hampshire, a base for submarine training. From here he wrote to Dickey:

At the moment I am living here, having been to sea at different times for the last two weeks, trying to draw interiors. Some of them may be successful, I hope, but conditions are difficult for work. It is awfully hot below when submarines dive and every compartment small and full of people at work. However, this is a change from destroyers and I enjoy the state of complete calm after the North Sea – there is no roll or movement at all in submarines, which is one condition in their favour – apart from the pecular submarine smell, the heat and the noise. There is something jolly good about it, if only I can manage it, a blue gloom with coloured lights and everyone in shirts and braces. People go to sleep in odd positions across tables.

In a letter to me he wrote:

There was a letter waiting for me here asking me to return to Chatham at once as the C. in C. wanted to have a talk about my drawings. I suspect he doesn't like them at all. It sounds like a rather difficult interview – but there it is. The Navy never were easy. . . . I've not done a great deal of work here yet, as submarine drawing is uphill work: however there is enough material for about six or seven lithographs. Don't you think that might be a good idea?

He went back to Chatham to see the admiral.

My C. in C. called me back to Chatham and read a lecture from his grand mahogany desk with the assurance of the Pope. I tried to shake him a little. He really needs 'a far less able pen than mine' but I couldn't quite say that to a C. in C. It was a curious interview and some very funny cross-talk. We parted on fairly good terms.

Eric was surprised therefore when he was told later by Dickey that the flag commander at Chatham had written an enthusiastic letter about the pictures, which he had seen at the War Artists' Exhibiton at the National Gallery. He was surprised because 'a very good many naval officers are dumb confronted with drawings of mine – or any drawings for that matter. I felt rather pleased that he liked them. It was very warming.'

But before he settled down to his sumbarine lithographs, Eric had one more series of watercolours to do – Admiral Sir William James had suggested his drawing the coastal defences at Newhaven, and this is where he went next. He had to go from Essex through London and Eastbourne. By now, the end of September, France had fallen, the raids on England had intensified and a German invasion seemed imminent. These descriptions of his journey and his time at Newhaven are all from letters to Tirzah:

Royal Naval Headquarters, Newhaven, Sussex

I have at last arrived here after an exciting but rather fruitless two days in London (and what nights!) and a day in Eastbourne. This was a bad dream. It was like the ruins of Pompeii, and both our families gone, the town all but empty – 60,000 people have left – I stayed at Elmwood Palace (the Garwood home) all dust-sheeted and moth-balled. Ethel was there and the gardeners' family living in the cellar and I think they were glad to see me. Grove Road is a bit of a mess, and the Art School entrance bombed. Your maternity home is bombed, and a tree outside down. All the windows of that nice white hotel in Burlington are broken, and the pier sawn in half. Mrs Church was the only resident I met, holding the fort in some wonderful uniform. I left Eastbourne after an early breakfast with a haunted feeling and could have run from the spot.

Here it is solid and naval and reassuring, and the people very friendly, though it is some way out of the town. London is unbelievable. I think Jim [Richards] is a hero to stick it – apart from anything else the nights are so very noisy. The place shakes with noise at times. Life is awful, romantic and nightmarish.

Here is a short letter because I've had a long day's work: not that very much is done, but a lot of exploring, and twice I've been hauled into the fort for enquiry. Now if the weather improves, I may do something. The scene is every bit as good as it used to be – with some modifications – there are air-raids, but what of it, and on the whole, things are very quiet.

It was fine to have ten letters this morning. What a record of adventure they mostly are!. . . I've to fetch a revolver from the barracks . . . all officers must carry tin hats and revolvers. I'm all for tin hats, with Germans just overhead as I work. They fly as they like.

c/o Mrs A'Brook, Grays, Western Road, Newhaven

I moved here because the R.N. Headquarters was too far away. We are bombed in the afternoon, about 3.30, but there are raids all day, and I find the tin hat lies heavy on the head. It seems to cram my neck into my coat like a tortoise. The pistol weighs pounds too. The weather has been perfect for work and all the usual old Raviliouses are now on the way, some bad, some good. I don't seem able to go quicker or slower, whatever is done – you buzz like a bee over it, obsessed for days. . . . Did you see Dickey's letter? I see the job may only last a bit longer so I may as well have a burst of work here, while I can. I like Newhaven.

With luck I ought to finish these drawings by Monday or Tuesday, and am going up to the cliffs twice a day like a man to the office.

It is a pretty quiet life here except for raids. There is so little navy to worry me and all the troops *inside* the fort. I draw in perfect peace of mind on this side the moat. It is simply wonderful. I could jump for joy sometimes.

Eric returned to Essex with seven paintings of Newhaven's pre-invasion – as they all thought – coastal defences.

Chapter 11

In September when Eric was at Portsmouth he had had a letter from Mr Dickey telling him that:

> strictly speaking, your six months' contract as a war artist finished on 10 August. We are not confident that the Treasury will make a fresh grant for war artists that will enable us to renew your contract for a further six months, which is the course the Artists Advisory Committee would favour.

Eric does not seem to have paid much attention, as it appeared to be only a question of pay, not of withdrawing permission to go on drawing and finishing what he had started.

However, by November the Treasury had decided to continue the grant for the artists, and Eric had written to say how pleased he would be to work for another six months after he had finished the submarine lithographs. He also suggested a trip to Iceland later, 'to draw the Royal Marines in hibernas, with duffel coats and perhaps those splendid plum skies'. He was now at home and working on the lithographs. On 29 October he wrote to me:

> The material at Portsmouth was awfully difficult to come by at all and of course really first rate and worth having a shot at, but the translation at home is slow work. I do feel very keen about it. This morning I heard that the committee want to make a children's painting book out of these submarine pictures to sell at a shilling, and print 10,000, so that the rising generation will clamour to go into the navy.

I suppose this would have been rather a risk financially; the committee decided not to undertake the painting book, and they suggested instead that Ravilious should find an outside publisher or printer to take it on. Some interested people were found and discussions begun. Eric had certainly imagined the lithographs being printed, as were his *High Street* lithographs, at the Curwen Press, but that was now out of the question: it had been damaged in an air-raid.

By 22 December nothing was settled, but Eric had found a printer in Ipswich, called W. S. Cowell:

> I've been so put about with these submarine pictures and even now have not begun work. The fourth publisher has failed – these people won't take a risk and make too many conditions; after endless consultations, they back out.
>
> So I'm doing the lithographs myself for fun. The bill is heavy but may be worth it in the long run, as the Leicester Galleries may show them. How fine not to have bloody publishers – and no children's book either. Ipswich will print the things and I start work tomorrow.

*Lithograph from the 'Submarine Series' – 'The Commander of a Submarine looking through the periscope' – 1941. 10¾" × 10¼".
Ravilious family*

Walrus Aircraft on Slipway
*Commissioned 1940. LD 1721. Watercolour. 19" × 21½".
Imperial War Museum, London*

'Tomorrow' was Christmas Eve, and Eric could write on 4 January in a letter to Diana Tuely:

I work away at these drawings of submarines, and have nearly finished three. It is fairly difficult and wholly absorbing trying to work out the superimpositions of five colours in all sorts of tones and textures and the rest. Lithography ink is beastly stuff, greasy and thick. The printer at Ipswich is very good and willing to make expensive experiments, and as I pay for the job instead of a publisher I rather want to try what experiments I can. The children's book idea is gone for good, and no bad thing either. Submarines aren't suitable for children.

By April the submarine pictures were done, but Eric felt that 'they were not as good as they ought to be. It is a pity. Some aren't bad! Perhaps lithography in five colours is too much and the result tends to be a chromo.' They were to be on sale at the Leicester galleries.

There was one more hurdle to be surmounted – the censor. At the end of March Eric wrote to Dickey, to whom he had sent the set of ten lithographs (the preliminary drawings had already been taken to show to one censor by Eric and passed by him).

Dear Dickey,

I was rather sorry to hear about the censor's decision and wish I had known about him earlier on. He seems to feel pretty strongly about it too. They seem to have come down heavily on those Newhaven drawings, not to mention the magnetic mine. I shall have quite a lot by the end of the war in their vaults and archives.

The winter of 1940–41 was the time of the London Blitz and the heavy raids on the ports and industrial centres of England. In November, Eric had had this sad letter:

Morley College, 61 Westminster Bridge Road, London SE1
5th November 1940

Dear Mr Ravilious,

I am most distressed to have to tell you that recently the main building of the College was completely destroyed by bombing, and your paintings have perished in the ruins.

The loss of your paintings is one part of a big tragedy, and I should like you to know how many people have expressed regret that they have gone. When they were painted we hoped, of course, that they would remain to delight many generations.

We hope that when the new Morley arises after the war we shall be able to have some sample of your work in memory of all you did for us.

Yours sincerely,
Eva M. Hubback, Principal

At Christmas there had been letters with news of old friends. A much diminished Royal College of Art had been evacuated to Ambleside. Percy Horton had gone with them, and wrote this account of 'Life and Hard Times in the Lakes' to Eric:

Some day I hope I shall be able to tell the full story of the RCA at Ambleside. It is a remarkable one and parts of it will make you roar with laughter. You should see Charlie Mahoney wrestling with the

Design for a lithograph from the 'Submarine Series' – 'Testing Davis apparatus in a 30' tank on H.M.S. Dolphin' – 1941.
National Maritime Museum, Greenwich

difficult problems that arise in the Queens Hotel – a place never designed for winter inhabitation. Burst pipes, choked-up lavatories, defective electric wiring and an almost impossible-to-organise system of numbering of rooms have been tackled by our very public-spirited Charles. This weekend 23 degrees of frost played havoc with water pipes and the lighting system failed completely. There is no general system of heating and the students had to grope their ways to their icy-cold bedrooms in complete darkness (they sleep four and five in a room with beds almost touching!).

John Nash, whose first assignment as a war artist had been to Plymouth, wrote that he had felt he couldn't go on with being a war artist, and he had decided to try for a real soldier's job. A Plymouth major had nearly got him one in the army, but it fell through and he had gone back to the observer post. John also mentioned that his brother Paul had been kicked out of the air force, which seemed fantastic to him – it must have been on grounds of ill-health.

There is this undated letter from Paul Nash to Eric; it must have been written either in the winter of 1939–1940 or late 1940:

106 Banbury Road, Oxford

Dear Eric,

I am painting a picture of Coastal Command and as I have been haunted for some time by the image of a Shortt Sunderland, I have begun to think of that noble beast as the best type of coast defence.

Now, although I could get all facilities necessary for becoming acquainted with S., I don't want to go off down the coast at this time of year with my kind of ailment – I have only just thrown off an attack of bronchitis. I thought of writing to you as someone most likely to be able to give me the information I want. Here is a rough note of the composition: [a diagram followed]

Encounter of S. with U boat just beyond Portland. Portland quarries and derricks. I've seen all that. What I want you to tell me is the colour of S. against a dark background with a low sun shining across the sea against the cliff. I *want S. to be almost white* in effect or *silver* white. As it would be moving swiftly its camouflage would not signify much. What are her usual colours and how nearly a great white object could it look. The same goes for the U boat. I've never seen one in life. I shall be able to visit some of the coast places in the Spring but I do need this information now. Can you help me? John turned up the other day, he said he had seen you. I haven't seen what you've been doing lately. I hope you are still as keen as ever.

All good wishes, Paul Nash

John Nash had news also of Barnett Freedman who 'still works on at vast paintings of guns and gun emplacements and seems really happy'.

Early in February, Eric had written a letter to Dickey at the Ministry of Information, which ended with this postscript:

P.S. I've just had a long visit from a Mr Gerald Holtom who seems very much to want designs for textiles for some Cotton Board. It would make a change to do this for a bit, and he assures me the whole thing is urgent and necessary. Do you know anything of this scheme? I said that it was a good idea which I would do if it were possible.

The committee agreed that Eric might in Mr Holtom's phrase 'postpone battle at sea for battle in export trade', and do some experiments in designing textiles before starting his next six months work for the Admiralty. He had still not quite finished the submarine lithographs.

Gerald Holtom had found a firm in Lancashire who produced handkerchiefs in very large quantities by a lithographic process. 'My proposal', he wrote to Eric, 'is that appropriate decorative handkerchiefs and scarves could be conveniently displayed at the travelling exhibitions of War Artists' and A.F.S. Artists' work in the U.S.A. I have spoken to Graham Sutherland who approves of the idea and I am writing to John Piper.' Gerald Holtom was even dreaming of a 'Victory Handkerchief'. Eric got as far as designing a children's handkerchief, in two blues on a white ground, on the theme of numbers one to ten – some samples were printed on white cotton, but it was not, I believe, produced in large quantities. A few of his designs were exhibited at the Colour Design and Style Centre, and one was bought by a Textile Firm. He wrote:

Work is slow, and there is a lot to be done before May when I go off again. The textile business is exciting, but unfamiliar and I don't pretend to have the hang of it yet, in spite of what Priestley calls an 'intelligent persistence'. All I seem to be doing is little clever piddling things – but why do women wear such tiny patterns? It confines a designer to the scale of a threepenny bit.

The family news was that Tirzah's third child had arrived on 1 April and, to the delight of both of them, was a girl. They decided to call her Anne.

Design for cotton handkerchief c1942. Ravilious family

At the end of April, at very short notice, they all moved from Castle Hedingham to a new house, but still in Essex. It was called Ironbridge Farm, at Shalford, near Braintree, and was in the valley of the Pant. The country and the river were looking lovely in the spring. The house, an old one, with very few conveniences, belonged to John Strachey, and the Raviliouses rented it on unusual terms. These were that half the year's rent – £70 – was to be paid in cash and the other half was to be paid with paintings up to the same value.

The next six months' work for the Admiralty was soon to start, and after his concentrated work at home, Eric found it stimulating to be painting again, this time at Dover. He went there for a spell in May, then back to Ironbridge. There were various delays about getting passes; on 24 June there was 'still no word from Dover', but he was off like a shot the moment it came; he described it in several letters:

August 19th, 1941

Dover is a good place. Except for shelling all the bombardment takes place on to the other side and is an extraordinary sight – Fireworks very clear and small. It is difficult to paint and I rather funk trying the dramatic again. . . . Last night when there was more shelling as well as wind and rain, it was pandemonium for a short time – The beaches are fuller than ever of curious flotsam and there was a skeleton under the cliff the other day; it was hard to tell, but I think it was a horse. There was a parachute and a lobster-pot with three crabs inside and a capital rowing boat by G. Renier of Guernsey, bright red and banana yellow – I wonder if somebody landed in it? It was so irresistible I made a tolerably good drawing of it, with some shelling going on at sea. This

129

Drift Boat
Commissioned 1940. LD
1590. Watercolour. 16¾″
× 20¾″.
Graves Art Gallery,
Sheffield

happened at the time – aimed at some trawlers – so I put it in, as inconspicuously as possible – Under the big cliff there is driftwood and logs and bits of plane, floats and rope ladders. Last year my landlord found a draper's roll there of black pinstripe suiting which he wears on Sundays now.

He moved his lodgings.

c/o Mrs Jarvest, 27 Old Folkestone Road, Dover

This is about a mile out of Dover, under the Shakespeare Cliff. . . . It is a nice place here; not too big and grand and majestically naval and I feel a stir in me that it is possible to really like drawing war activities. The town is almost empty and lots of sad ruins and I feel tempted to try some of the wallpapery interiors, in fact will do so later on. There are a few beauties. It is much livelier where I am now, also more on the spot for drawing. I got up in the night to have a look at the shelling from the Cliff and it is an appalling noise but that is about all. It did no harm. There is a great flash and explosion on the French side and then about 80 seconds later the shell lands in the sea, and a second bang and the sky lights up – I doubt if I can draw this – it is too formless. I'll try it very small and see what happens.

There must have been some intensive bombardments, as Tirzah was writing to him, 'I wonder what you were doing while they were shelling Dover. I hope you are still intact. Luckily I only hear about these things a long time after they have occurred.'

John Nash, no longer a war artist, but now on Commander in Chief's staff at Rosyth in a different capacity, had told Eric that he would find good subjects to paint in the east coast ports of Scotland. Eric had sailed past them and under the Forth Bridge on his way to Norway, and was delighted at the idea, which was also aproved. On 6 October Eric wrote to the Ministry of Information.

I heard from the Admiralty this morning about going up to Rosyth. This is good news and I am packing to go off as soon as possible. There were a good many people there whose permission was needed first apparently.
Gleadowe has given me a magnificent new Pass.

The Nashes had taken a cottage near Dunfermline and Eric much enjoyed staying with them, being taken round by John, and having them as a base to come back to, between visits to draw the docks and the Forth Bridge, and a stay of a few days aboard H.M.S. *Killarney*, and on May and other islands in the Firth of Forth. From R.N. Signal Station, May Island, he wrote to Tirzah:

I've landed here by way of a destroyer – and an R.A.F. launch – and am now living with this small naval mess, five officers and a few ratings. They are all very nice people. The island is rocky and rolling and wild, in peacetime a bird sanctuary. Hoodie crows and golden-crested wrens are about; I wish you could see the island. You would love it. There is the oldest beacon – 1636 – in the centre (you light a fire on the roof of a thing like a large dovecot) and the turf is just like a pile carpet. They took me to the lighthouse lantern this morning. I've just been entranced with the place all day and explored without working so must have an early bed (one game of darts) and work early tomorrow.

R.N.A.S. Sick Bay, Dundee
Commissioned 1940. LD 1719. Watercolour. 19¼" × 21½".
Imperial War Museum, London

But he stayed longest at an R.N.A. station at Dundee and wrote this about it to Dickey in November:

H.M.S. *Ambrose*, Mayfield Hostel, Ferry Road, Dundee

This is an excellent place for work, the address a Fleet Air Arm mess. I spend my time drawing sea planes and now and again they take me up; this morning rather uncomfortably in the tail, but it was worth it for the view. I do very much enjoy drawing these queer flying machines and hope to produce a set of aircraft paintings. I hope Paul N. hasn't already painted Walrus's – what I like about them is that they are comic things with a strong personality like a duck, and designed to go slow. You put your head out of the window and it is no more windy than a train.

There is more about Eric at Dundee:

These planes and pilots are the best things I have come across since this job began. They are sweet and have no nonsense (naval traditional nonsense and animal pride): they help in all sorts of ways and take me up when they can. I must say it is most enjoyable. . . . It is a joke dressing up with flying suit, parachute, Mae West and all and climbing in over the nose. Some time this week they promise a trip in the rear-gunner's cockpit which is uncomfortable but has the best view: the only drawback is that I have to do a number of simple (?) mechanical things with hatches when the sea-plane comes down on the water. How trusting they are!

Surprisingly, perhaps, Eric had no instinct for machines; for instance he never learnt to drive a car.

From now on his keenest interest was in painting aeroplanes, and eventually *from* them.

He got back from Scotland about ten days before Christmas to find all the children with whooping cough. The worst was over but the baby and James had had it badly. Luckily, Tirzah had been able to get a nurse, but it must have been very difficult, particularly in a house which was really only suitable for summer living. This was again a very cold winter.

John and Myfanwy Piper had been coming to stay for Christmas, but this was put off. There had been the usual exchange of presents and news. Here is part of a letter written to Eric by Tom Hennell:

Dear Eric

It was very good to get your letter: and I hope soon to see your new war record paintings. I wish you would paint in oils on the sheets of the linen scrap-book, for I think it would suit you. It's a bit too smooth for my taste. I remember a painting you were doing at Bardfield in 1928 [Edward Bawden thinks this date must be a mistake; it must have been later] of parachutes descending, in oil on balloon cloth – surely a foretaste of present events.

Graham Sutherland, who lives near here, was doing a series of kettles on the fire last Christmas; and now he is painting foundries, boilers and cauldrons of molten steel – and so his progress has been on similar lines to Stephenson's who made the 'Rocket'.

He paints on a smooth canvas, sometimes sprinkling a little sand. What I should like to understand and practise, is the use of a preparation under one's final painting (whether in oils or water colour) which might give tone and unity to it. I think you do this in watercolour. Your Welsh mountain and sheep (David Jones' farm) hangs framed in my book room and has been very greatly admired.

This letter was accompanied by a pot of honey, 'against the whooping cough'.

There was soon to be a long letter from Edward Bawden.

Public Relations Unit, G.H.Q. Middle East
Feb. 21, 1942

My dear Eric

If I make haste to answer the letter of yours I received this morning you will get something in return to show how much I appreciate the flattering remarks about my work and the news of yourself, Tirzah, and the multiplying family.

It is better for you to remain in Scotland – foul though the weather may be – than to come to Africa. You might be disappointed, or at least unsympathetic; 'disappointed' is not the word because I believe you have a clearer idea than I had of what the Middle East might be like. In the first place there is an awful lot of sand. Along the coastal belt of the Mediterranean rain is frequent at this time of year – a cold heavy rain. A bad combination is rain, an icy wind, and a sandstorm; a sandstorm by itself is depressing enough. The signs appear about nine when the sky shows a mousey colour creeping above the horizon, soon a wind is felt which increases rapidly in force; this blows sand along the ground in long ropey lines; often it creates the illusion that wisps of smoke are escaping from the infernal regions – the hard stony desert terrain might be a thin volcanic crust cracking like ice to allow wisps of smoke and steam to escape. It is a strange illusion and quite perfect. I do not exaggerate when I say that I have been fascinated watching it though my heart sank at the thought of yet another day completely wasted. The sand rises slowly, for an hour it may be only a few inches, a foot, or up to the waist – you have time to get back to a tent or into a truck to roll head and heels into a blanket and pass the time philosophically.

I believe I have already said enough to convince you that a certain part of Essex is by comparison a landscape painter's paradise: it is – make no error about it. If my *aide de camp*, Mohammed Ahmed, came to Essex I expect he would see little except for a blur of green. We know what to look for – a rabbit flick, the scurry of a stoat, primroses in ditches, or dog roses in hedgerows are caught by the corner of an eye, but Mohammed would not see them. So do I find it here – I look and search carefully and see something interesting only by patience or accident.

I should like to see your work. Charlotte writes enthusiastically about it, and Anthony Gross gives me a skimpy idea of what it is like. It's strange to unseal lips after nineteen months and talk again of painting and painters. Give my love to Tirzah and the family. Write again if you can – letters are very infrequent and mean more to me than they ever did at home.

Love, and best wishes, and success,
Edward

Edward had been having an adventurous time as a war artist with the army. Going first to France, he got back from Dunkirk, and was next sent to the Middle East. From Cairo he went to Khartoum and Rosaires, eventually joining a camel cavalcade of Sudanese and Ethiopians tramping to Addis Ababa. It was here that he had made the drawings of Menelek's Palace that Eric had so specially admired at the National Gallery Exhibition.

Edward went on further expeditions by land and sea, culminating in a shipwreck off Lagos and five days in a lifeboat until he was picked up by a French Vichy warship and deposited in a prisoner of war camp in Morocco. Rescued later by the Americans, he got back to England by way of the United States, too late for him ever to see Eric again.

Because he was so keen to draw more aeroplanes, Gleadowe had arranged a meeting between Eric and Group Captain Lord Willoughby de Broke, the Air Ministry representative on the War Artists' Advisory Committee. He gave Eric a wonderful lunch at Boodles and was full of good suggestions for the next trip. Lysanders were the first prospect with the Coastal Command (Sunderlands and Catalinas) to follow. Ireland was mentioned as a possible place to visit, but Russia was out of the question. Eric felt this was a pity, 'as they have planes on skis there; he clung to a hope that there might be a chance later on to go there in some round-about way.

The Lysander aeroplanes he was to draw next were at an R.A.F. station in the Plain of York; after delays and changes of plan by the Air Ministry, Eric arrived there on 1 March, and was delighted with the place, the people and the aeroplanes. He had started to draw them when there was a sudden summons home – Tirzah, who had been in hospital for a few days in February for a small operation and had returned looking well, had now been told by her doctor that she needed to have another and much more serious operation at once in the Braintree hospital. Eric got back to Essex as quickly as war travelling made possible. The operation was pronounced successful, though Tirzah had a difficult time and needed blood transfusions. Eric was given a fortnight's leave. At the hospital, he found Tirzah, 'pale but quite cheerful', and he took in reproductions of Matisses and Utrillos for the mantelpiece, to offset 'Betwixt two Fires' – Matisse was strong meat for the nurses, who thought that Eric had painted them.

> Did I say James had measles? Tirzah's mother has come to hold the fort and does so very well indeed. I'm ashamed I used to dislike her so much at Eastbourne. Now I get on with her perfectly well. . . . We are too busy to think about anything but food and fires and measles, doctors and black-outs and ducks and hens. . . . As a sort of gesture against calamities I'm trying to paint in oils – I don't know what will come of it.

Reading that now, it strikes a chill, and in a later letter he said: 'My oil-painting came to nothing – it didn't seem to strike roots at all.'

A month after her operation he reported that Tirzah was out of hospital, but needing a complete rest. Her mother took her and the children back to Eastbourne, where they could all benefit from sea air. A year earlier when a German invasion threatened, the authorities had urged everyone who could to leave the town. The Garwoods had found a haven with relations in Worcestershire, but it had been difficult, and they were glad to be back in their own home, in spite of fairly frequent hit-and-run air-raids on the town.

Eric had been able to arrange to paint at a nearby airfield at Debden instead of York, so that he could cycle back to Ironbridge if he were needed. His next move was to the R.A.F. station at Sawbridgeworth in Hertfordshire. These descriptions of his work there are taken from letters to various people:

Here I am committed to drawing planes for some time, and find it slow work because conditions aren't easy. Everything is fluid and shifting and I work in feverish haste and then dislike the result, or, take my time and the subject matter just leaves the field. It is possible I may go up to Stratford-on-Avon in about a month. But this plan hasn't been decided on and I don't feel too sure about being able to draw giant bombers. They are such repellent things.

And a little later, 'How I've been working this last few weeks, successful drawings being in the usual proportion of one out of two or three – if only aeroplanes weren't all so alike and so edgy and tinny. The Tiger Moth is the perfect plane for drawing.'

In a letter making an appointment to see Dickey at the Ministry of Information, he wrote:

The idea is to return to Sawbridgeworth for some flying, as it would be a good plan to try some drawing from the air in this weather.

Now for some work and jolly hard work for a bit because it starts from almost nothing you could call solid or substantial. Air pictures don't have enough horizontals and verticals; they are all clouds and patterned fields and bits and pieces of planes. In time something could

Tiger Moth
Commissioned 1941. LD 2130. Watercolour. 17¾" × 21½".
The Trustees of the Tate Gallery, London

135

be done I think all the same.

As he explored these new subjects, Eric's paintings were growing in sureness, each one a distillation of a very personal vision.

Eric was always aware how few artists are able to keep alive the excitement of the first flowering of their work, and how soon it can sink into dullness. Edward Bawden remembers how Eric in his middle twenties spoke of the early thirties as the difficult time. (On his thirty-fourth birthday, Tirzah had noted a rare occurence in her diary: 'Eric drunk and disorderly.') He was now in his late thirties. He would be thirty-nine on 22 July. In a letter to me, he showed he still felt the pressure of time: 'What do you think I wonder about that depressing theory of mine about middle-aged painters? Anyway let's not start applying it yet. I would very much like to be the camel that gets through the Eye of the Needle if I knew how to set about it.'

Except for his work, it was a sad and difficult time for Eric and his family. Eric's mother, of whom he was so fond, had died the year before, and his father was very lonely and unhappy. That spring he was in hospital in Eastbourne and on the danger list. Tirzah, herself in Eastbourne, wrote to tell Eric this, and here is his answer from the R.A.F. station at Sawbridgeworth:

My darling Tush,
What a day it has been – I'm in the throes of work here and unwilling to leave it, but this news of my poor old father is worrying. However send me a wire if I ought to come down. It is a bit unnerving for you, all this coping with emergency – how they do seem to dog our steps so that I begin to hesitate at opening letters these days and brace myself for the expected news. . . .
Will you post this letter to my father as I don't know his address? My love to you and to our Anneandjames. [His elder boy, John, was now at a boarding school.] God bless them.
Eric

He did manage to visit his father, who survived that illness.

The last time that I saw Eric was at the beginning of July. He had been sent to draw at an R.N.A. training station at Westonzoyland on the Somerset coast. He had suggested coming to Bath on his way back to London; we walked over the hills outside Bath and had a picnic in a valley near Charlcombe. It gradually came out that he had been deeply disturbed by something that had happened while he was watching a training session of the new young pilots. Their seaplanes were following each other in turn, flying in a straight line over the sea. Suddenly one of them lost control, and dived nose down into the sea. But the others were not allowed to stop. The exercise had to go on.

Eric had talked to and liked the young man so suddenly drowned before his eyes. He couldn't forget the shock of it. I remember him almost shouting, 'I hate the idea' – of death he must have meant: his own?

Since student days Eric had loved the watercolours of Francis Towne, that eighteenth-century artist who had painted glaciers and snow peaks in Switzerland. This was one of the reasons why his imagination was so taken with the idea of painting in Iceland. But even more, it was that magical experience of sailing up into the Arctic Circle and seeing the midnight sun that had left him feeling that for him the North was the Promised Land.

So he reminded the authorities of his suggestion of going to paint in Iceland. Lord Willoughby de Broke hoped to be able to arrange it; on 22 July Eric wrote to Dickey:

> I may go off to Iceland if Lord Willoughby de Broke can arrange that. He thought it a good idea to fly there. Will you be seeing him in the next week or two? I'd like to visit the Norwegian squadron, but some kind of general pass would be even better, if it can be managed without too much trouble.

The Norwegian Squadron, stationed in Iceland, flew their own Northrops aeroplanes, which Eric was very keen to see and to draw.

To the great regret of all the war artists, Dickey was leaving his job at the Ministry of Information. He gave a farewell dinner party which was a great success. At the end Eric got carried away in a taxi with the Kenneth Clarks, Henry Moore, Barnett Freedman and Graham Sutherland to the Hollybush to drink shandies, and then to Kenneth Clark's for more. It was a merry party. 'Lots of clever talk of course. How I enjoyed it,' he wrote afterwards.

On 4 August, 'No phone call yet from the Admiralty.' But later in August he wrote from London to Tirzah:

> I went to Northwood and to the Air Ministry twice, so things ought to be really moving at last, though it will be a passenger plane from Scotland and not a bomber – so much the better. I was going to the dinner and a car stopped. Who should get out but James Fisher (at the Zoo, you remember him at Jim's party?) [He looked after the first panda when it came to the zoo, driving it every day there in his car.] He gave me lots of information about Iceland and some introductions to naturalists there. I want to see him again.
>
> x x x Eric.
>
> I go off probably the end of next week.

There is a postcard sent by Eric to Tirzah from Prestwick on 27 August, saying 'It is calm and fine here with no wind and I hope very much we go tomorrow'.

They did.

The telegram came on 5 September, followed by this letter next day:

> In confirmation of the Admiralty's telegram despatched today, I am commanded by My Lords Commissioners of the Admiralty of State that they have been informed that your husband, temporary Captain Eric Ravilious, Royal Marines, had been reported as missing since Wednesday last, 2nd September, 1942, when the aircraft in which he was a passenger failed to return from a patrol.
>
> My Lords desire me to express to you their deep sympathy in the great anxiety which this news must cause you and to assure you that any further information which can be obtained will be immediately communicated.

Here are the details of what had happened as reported to Lord Willoughby de Broke at the Air Ministry who also wrote to Tirzah.

R.A.F., Iceland
September 6th, 1942

I am sorry that the visit of Captain Ravilious to this country has ended so tragically. He had intended, he informed me on his arrival, to remain here until practically Christmas and having introduced him all round people were looking forward to his proposed stay with them.

He went to Kaldarnes, which is one of our stations, where I think he was going to remain for about a fortnight. On the night of 1st of September one of our aircraft was reported missing from an operational job and a search by three aircraft was organised at dawn on the 2nd to sweep the area 300 miles to seawards. Ravilious went in one of these, which happened to be the Air Sea Rescue craft, no doubt to use the rescue as a subject for one of his drawings. From the time of take-off of his aircraft until now, we have heard nothing more.

Further, the most exhaustive search, lasting four days has been carried out and I am afraid we must now give up all hope and assume that they are lost. The American Army have been grand in the way they have combed the whole of the South West Peninsula of this Island on foot all this time, whilst in co-operation with the air, we have also searched the sea, but with no result.

We are all very distressed at these two losses as you will appreciate.

K. B. Lloyd

Tirzah, I think, realized from the first that there could not really be any hope that Eric would be found.

A week later this letter from Eric came for Tirzah. It had been written in pencil on 1 September, his first and only letter from Iceland.

Care of R.A.F., Iceland
Sunday 31st Aug.

My darling Tush,

I do hope you feel well again. It was a comfort to know of your plans and that Evelyn would be there for a month. Was there a heat wave in Essex? I left Scotland just as it was really hot and a beach scene like pre-war Eastbourne. The journey here was very good, [censored word] of perfectly calm flying – no tea of course but a dinner to make up for it on arrival. Yesterday was spent making the usual visits and they were all very hopeful and nice people. I was taken to lunch in the town to eat Icelandic food and the spread was unbelievable, like Fortnum at his best, caviar and pâté, cheese, goodness know what. You assemble a pyramid of all this on the plate and drink milk with it. The shops have rather nice things, I see, though pretty expensive. Would you like a pair of gloves – sealskin with the fur on the back – but what size shall I buy? Draw round your hand on the writing paper. I saw a splendid narwhal horn yesterday, delicately spiralled and about six foot high as far as I remember. Perhaps if I go to Greenland it may be possible to find one. It is a beautiful thing, heavy of course and quite useless. No plane would take it I'm afraid. I am promised an expedition to see the geysers next week. They seem to need soap to start them off. It is jolly cold here, and windy and rainy too, like January, after the hot sun in Scotland: no place for you at all, though you would like the country, especially the flowers and the seals. I hope to visit them soon. I might collect some flowers for you and shells for John, if there are such things, but the weather is too rough to go and look for them. I wish I had brought Di's pillow as there isn't one here. One must travel with that and looking glass for shaving and a towel. I shall buy them later. There are no sheets either but I don't mind that at all. I sleep well without.

Is Edward home yet? And how is my father? I will write to him when there is a chance. All my love to James and John and Anne and I hope James doesn't mind being away from the family. Give my love too to Ariel and Evelyn. I mean to write to John Crittall and lots of people – but explain to them how difficult writing is on these trips.

We flew over that mountain country that looks like craters on the moon and it looked just like those photographs the M. of Information gave me, with shadows very dark and shaped like leaves. It is a surprising place. There are no mosquitoes so far but clouds of dust make up for their absence. The rain has laid the dust a bit today.

Write to this address all the time, as they will forward letters, and I shall be travelling about the island a lot; of course remember that letters are censored.

Get well won't you Tusho and eat all you can. A pity you couldn't live in this town and get fat, which is certainly what would happen if you gave your mind to it.

Let me have the introduction to Lt. Benham if it turns up. I will go and see him. Goodbye darling. Take care of yourself. My love (and gratitude for coming like that at a minute's notice) to Evelyn.

Eric

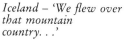

Iceland – 'We flew over that mountain country. . .'

Chronology

1903   22 July: born in Acton.

1914   Went to Eastbourne Grammar School.

1919   December: takes Cambridge Senior Local Examination. Awarded Scholarship to Eastbourne School of Art.

1922   Autumn: began Diploma course at Royal College of Art.

1924   Summer: passes Diploma Examination with distinction. Awarded Design School Travelling Scholarship to Italy.

1925   Last year at Royal College. Shares studio with Douglas Percy Bliss in Redcliffe Road, London. September: began teaching part-time at Eastbourne School of Art. October: proposed for membership of the Society of Wood Engravers by Paul Nash and accepted.

1926   Designs production of *The Careful Wife* staged by Eastbourne Art School students. Meets Tirzah Garwood, a new student, and is first taken to the Garwood home. Wood Engravings for *Desert* by Martin Armstrong (Jonathan Cape).

1927   Living in Eastbourne with his parents. Engravings for *A Ballad upon a Wedding* by Sir John Suckling and *The Twelve Moneths* by Nicholas Breton (Golden Cockerel Press). October: exhibited with Edward Bawden and Douglas Percy Bliss at St George's Gallery, London.

1928   Morley College Murals: Ravilious's and Bawden's scale drawings sent to William Rothenstein in June/July; commission confirmed 10 July. Work started at the College in September.

1929   Various wood engravings published: Lanston Monotype Corporation *Almanack*; 'The Song of the Three Holy Children' in *The Apocrypha* (Cresset Press); 'Doctor Faustus Conjuring Mephistophilis' in *The Legion Book* (Cassells); *The Atrocities of the Pirates* by Aaron Smith (Golden Cockerel Press); and a variety of wood engravings in *The Woodcut*.

1930   January: engagement to Tirzah Garwood. February: Morley College unveiled by Stanley Baldwin. Portrait of Edward Bawden in his studio. 'Tennis' panels for Sir Geoffrey Fry's Portman Court flat. Two wood engravings for *Elm Angel* by Walter de la Mare (Faber & Faber). 5 July: wedding. After honeymoon in Cornwall Eric and Tirzah moved to 5 Stratford Road, Kensington, and later to Weltje Road, Hammersmith. Eric began teaching part-time at Royal College and Ruskin School of Art, Oxford. Autumn: began work on Shakespeare's *Twelfth Night* for the Golden Cockerel Press, commissioned by Robert Gibbings.

1931   Golden Cockerel Press: three engravings for the *Prospectus* and designs for *Twelfth Night*.

1932   *Twelfth Night* published. March: decorating Brick House, Great Bardfield, with Edward Bawden. April: *Room and Book* exhibition organised by Paul Nash at Zwemmer's; exhibits *Cactus House Design*. Cover for Golden Cockerel Press *Prospectus*. *Winters of Content* by Osbert Sitwell (Duckworth), cover and frontispiece. *Consequences* (Golden Cockerel Press), frontispiece and title page.

1933   *The Famous Tragedy of the Rich Jew of Malta* (Golden House Press), four wood engravings. 29 vignettes for *54 Conceits* by Martin Armstrong, (Martin Secker Ltd). 1933 Lanston Monotype Corporation calendar. 10 April: arrived with Tirzah at the Midland Railway Hotel, Morecambe to paint murals in the circular tearoom and bar. Hotel opened on 12 July. August and September: painting at Great Bardfield with the Bawdens. Autumn: working mainly in London – *The Stork*, and *November 5th – Bonfire Night*. 24 November – 16 December: first one-man exhibition at Zwemmer's.

1934   Spring: first visits to Furlongs in the South Downs; *Mount Caburn, Alpha Cement Works, Furlongs*, etc. March: return to Morecambe to try to restore murals. April: Colwyn Bay Pier Pavilion. Murals painted in restored interior with Mary Adshead. Spring-Summer: bought and restored two caravans at Furlongs. Summer: screen for Sir Geoffrey Fry. September: rented Bank House at Castle Hedingham.

1935   John Ravilious born. *The Hansom Cab and The Pigeons* by L.A.G. Strong (Golden Cockerel Press). Other wood engravings included: *Thrice Welcome* (British Railways Board); advertisements for Green Line Buses; designs for John Murray; Dent's Everyman Library, and Duckworth's New Readers Library; Double Crown Club Annual Dinner menu. Selection of wood engravings published in first issue of *Signature*. August: painting expedition with Edward Bawden; stayed at the Hope Inn, Newhaven. First meeting with Josiah Wedgwood; trial pottery designs.

1936   *Poems by Thomas Hennell* (Oxford University Press). 5–29 February: second one-man exhibition at Zwemmer's. Dunbar Hay Ltd opened; wood engraving for shop's trade card. To Stoke-on-Trent to discuss pottery designs with Wedgwood, particularly the Edward VIII Coronation Mug put into production later that year.

October: to Stoke again with Cecilia Dunbar Kilburn.
Country Walks (London Transport Board).
1937 Gave up teaching.
The Country Life Cookery Book by Ambrose Heath.
Paris International Exhibition: *Tennis* exhibit and catalogue cover for British Pavilion.
Began work on *High Street* and *The Natural History of Selborne*.
Winter: visits to John and Christine Nash in Buckinghamshire and Diana and Clissold Tuely in Kent.
1938 *The Natural History of Selborne* (Nonesuch Press).
Spring: painted Breconshire landscapes at Capel-y-Ffin.
Summer: Kent Coast: *Rye Harbour, Room at the 'William the Conqueror'*; visit to Aldeburgh: *Bathing Machines, Lifeboat*.
November: painting expedition to Bristol with John Nash: *Bristol Quay*.
Winter-Spring 1939: painted around Newhaven.
1939 March: visit to Normandy.
11 May – 3 June: shared exhibition at Arthur Tooth's.
Summer: began series of chalk figures.
James Ravilious born.
September: war declared. Volunteered to work at Hedingham Observation Post.
December: offered position as Official War Artist by the Admiralty.
1940 February: six-month contract as Official War Artist began. Posted to Chatham: *Ship's Screw on a Railway Truck*.
March: Sheerness and Whitstable: *Barrage Balloons outside a British Port, Dangerous Work at Low Tide*.
April: Grimsby: *Grimsby Trawlers*.
May–June: with H.M.S. Highlander to Norway and the Arctic Circle: *Leaving Scapa Flow, Norway 1940, Ark Royal in Action* etc.
July: first exhibition of War Artists' work at National Gallery.
Summer: drawings of submarine interiors at Portsmouth and H.M.S. Dolphin, Hampshire.
September – October: watercolours of coastal defences near Newhaven and Eastbourne.
November: Morley College destroyed in bombing.
1941 Spring: submarine lithographs printed and put on sale at Leicester Galleries, London.
Textile designs for Cotton Board.
Anne Ravilious born; Eric's mother Emma died.
Move from Castle Hedingham to Ironbridge Farm.
Summer: Dover: *Shelling at Night*.
Autumn: Scotland. Stayed with John and Christine Nash. Painted in Firth of Forth: *Channel Fisher, R.N.A.S. Sick Bay, Dundee*.
1942 Spring: with R.A.F. in Yorkshire, Essex and Hertfordshire: painting Lysanders and Tiger Moths.

July: R.N.A.S. training station, Weston-zoyland, Somerset.
28 August: stationed at Kaldarnes, Iceland.
2 September: went on an air-sea rescue mission which failed to return. Reported as missing, presumed dead.

Exhibitions

Eric Ravilious had three major exhibitions of his watercolours during his lifetime, the first two one-man exhibitions at the Zwemmer Gallery in 1933 and 1936, and the last a shared exhibition at Arthur Tooth's in 1939. The works exhibited are as follows:

Zwemmer Gallery, 1933
1   Engines in Winter (10 guineas)
2   Funnel and Roller (10 guineas)
3   Tractor (10 guineas)
4   Engine Yard (10 guineas)
5   Buoys and Grappling Hook (10 guineas)
6   Apples and Walnuts (10 guineas)
7   Field Elm (10 guineas)
8   Newt Pond (10 guineas)
9   River Thames (12 guineas)
10 Marrow Bed (8 Guineas)
11 Pond: Half Past Seven (9 guineas)
12 Village School (9 guineas)
13 Great Saling (9 guineas)
14 Sandpit (9 guineas)
15 Prospect From An Attic (15 guineas)
16 Farmyard (10 guineas)
17 Pink Farm (9 guineas)
18 Drought (10 guineas)
19 Hawser (10 guineas)
20 The Stork, Hammersmith (12 guineas)
21 February Landscape (10 guineas)
22 Walls and Sheds (9 guineas)
23 Tilty (10 guineas)
24 Willows (10 guineas)
25 Chapels (8 guineas)
26 Lindsell (10 guineas)
27 High Street (12 guineas)
28 Afternoon in the Fields (10 guineas)
29 Flags (15 guineas)
30 Fireworks (15 guineas)
31 Rainscombe (12 guineas)
32 Marlborough Downs (not for sale)
33 Huish Gap (12 guineas)
34 Strawberry Bed (not for sale)
35 November 5th (25 guineas)
36 High Tide (15 guineas)
37 Twelve Months (Engravings for the Kynoch Press Calendar). Edition of Twelve (set: 5 guineas)

Zwemmer Gallery 1936
All the works exhibited were priced at 12 guineas each
1   Kirby Hall Fields
2   Dolly Engine
3   Coalyard

Since Ravilious died there have been three major exhibitions devoted to his work, each of which was accompanied by an important catalogue. These are as follows:

Eric Ravilious Memorial Exhibition Towner Art Gallery, Eastbourne, and Brighton Art Gallery, 1948. This exhibition was used as the basis for a smaller Arts Council exhibition, 1948–9

Eric Ravilious, 1903–1942 Graves Art Gallery, Sheffield, 1958. Catalogue introduction by Richard Seddon

Eric Ravilious, 1903–1942 The Minories, Colchester, 1972. Catalogue preface by Michael Chase and notes by Edward Bawden, Douglas Percy Bliss, Cecilia Lady Sempill, Helen Binyon and John Nash

Bibliography

Beckinsale, Mary, 'The Work of Eric Ravilious (1903–1942), Its Origins and Originality'. Unpublished thesis presented to Cambridge University, 1958

Carrington, Noel, 'Eric Ravilious', *Graphis* 16, pp 430–5, Zurich 1946

Constable, Freda, *The England of Eric Ravilious*, Scolar Press 1982

Gilmore, Patricia, *Artists at Curwen*, Curwen Press, 1977.

Gooden, R. Y., 'Eric Ravilious as a Designer', *Architectural Review* pp 155–61, December 1943

Harling, Robert, *Notes on the Wood Engravings of Eric Ravilious*, Ariel Book on the Arts, Faber and Faber 1946

O'Connor, John, 'Eric Ravilious: A Recollection by one of his pupils', *Cockalorum* pp 82–3, Golden Cockalorum Press 1950

Richards, J.M., *The Wood Engravings of Eric Ravilious*, Lion and Unicorn Press, 1972

Sandford, Christopher, 'In Memoriam', 1948 BBC talk given with Tirzah Ravilious, published in *Cockalorum*, pp 73–81, Golden Cockerel Press 1950

Simon, Oliver (ed.), 'The Printed and Published Wood Engravings of Eric Ravilious', *Signature* 1, pp 30–41, 1935

Index

Italic numerals indicate black
and white illustrations;
bold italic numerals indicate
colour illustrations.

CLEVELAND INSTITUTE OF ART GUND LIBRARY
Eric Ravilious : memoir of an a
N6797 .R9 1983

DATE DUE

GAYLORD

PRINTED IN U.S.A.